A HIS

OF

THE FEUD

BETWEEN THE

HILL AND EVANS PARTIES

OF GARRARD COUNTY, KY.

THE MOST EXCITING TRAGEDY EVER ENACTED ON THE BLOODY
GROUNDS OF KENTUCKY.

BY LIEUT. J. J. THOMPSON.

———

CINCINNATI:
PUBLISHED BY U. P. JAMES.

TO THE

GOOD, GREAT, AND CHIVALRIC PEOPLE

OF

KENTUCKY,

THIS LITTLE VOLUME

IS RESPECTFULLY DEDICATED BY

THE AUTHOR.

PREFACE.

WESTERN MILITARY INSTITUTE,
Tyree Springs, Tenn., June, 1854.

THE public may perhaps think that I am imprudent in having so much to do with a difficulty which has caused so much bloodshed. But the fact that I record the events of the Fued, need not necessarily involve me in its intricate meshes.

It must be considered that I do not hold myself accountable for the facts herein contained, since I received them personally from Dr. Evans. My getting the facts of the history is purely accidental. Our Institute having been disbanded at Drennon Springs, Ky., on account of sickness, I went down to Garrard county to spend a short time with my relatives. I had learned much of this Fued from the gossip of the county, and naturally became curious to know more. I had the fortune to become acquainted with one of Dr. Evans's sons, who recounted to me some of the thrilling events. He likewise informed me that Dr. Evans had most of the facts reduced to writing; whereupon I wrote a note to him, requesting an account of the entire Fued, (should it meet his approbation,) and stating that I desired to build from it a romance in the Spanish language. He came up to see me in a few days, and said he would give the narrative only on one condition—that I should write it in the English language. With the advice of my friends, I consented to do so.

I am aware that this history is imperfect, inasmuch as it is taken from only one of the parties; to render it complete, we should have to obtain a knowledge of the secret plans and designs of the other party, which was impracticable; for Dr. Hill's whereabouts is not known. But the facts of which we are in possession are true. The reception of facts upon the evidence of testimony is referable chiefly to three heads : that the individual has had sufficient opportunity of ascertaining the facts ; that we have confidence in his power of judging of their accuracy; and that we believe him to be an honest witness. With respect to the first two elements there can be no doubt, and to substantiate the third, a number of certificates will be found in the Appendix from some of the most reliable men in the country. And it is scarcely probable that Dr. Evans would tell that which his neighbors would rise up and contradict. There remains one other source of error — that I may have misunderstood Dr. Evans, or received ideas from his words which he did not intend to convey. But this is a mere probability; and should it prove a reality, the people have a sufficient sense of honor and justice to pass it by. Let it be understood, however, that I have not exclusively used Dr. Evans's words in many instances, but have clothed his ideas in my own words.

From the fact that the Hills appear to great disadvantage, some persons may, perhaps, accuse me of being partial to Dr. Evans. But they cannot make this accusation, if they pay attention to the *facts* — facts speak louder than words. Should I be partial to either, nature would favor the Hills, for I am distantly related to them through the Pollard line. I have much favored the Hills by assuming in many places a calm and argumentative style. What I have said about either party would have been said about any other under similar circumstances.

I am much indebted to my esteemed friend, Major T. C. Downie, of this Institute, for his kind advice and aid in compiling this little work.

Should the public demand a second edition, and the Hill party produce facts to place them more favorably before the world, I shall be happy to do them justice, and receive the requisite information at my residence in Brooksville, Noxubee county, Mississippi.

J. J. THOMPSON.

CERTIFICATES.

I do not know that it is essentially necessary to produce certificates of Dr. Evans's character, but should any one doubt his veracity, and thus doubt the truth of this narrative, he can find sufficient proof in the following. I have many others, but these few will suffice. They are given by some of the first citizens of the county, in whom unlimited confidence may be placed. I am personally acquainted with nearly all these gentlemen, and can vouch for them

---

STATE OF KENTUCKY, *Garrard County,* (*To wit,*)

I, James H. Letcher, of the county and State aforesaid, do state that I have been acquainted with Dr. Hezekiah Evans since the year 1816 — he and I have resided in this county ever since. From my long acquaintance with said Evans, and having frequent business transactions with him, I can say with confidence that he is very prompt and punctual in all his dealings, and a man of integrity and veracity, and I believe this to be his character with all his acquaintances, except his personal enemies. I should readily believe any statement he would make on oath or otherwise.

I was for a number of years clerk of the Garrard county court, for several years a justice of the peace, and for three years past, judge of the county court.

May 4th, 1854.   JAMES H. LETCHER.

Lancaster, Ky, May 4th, 1854.

I certify that I have known Dr. Hezekiah Evans for the last fourteen years, two years of which time I was deputy sheriff of Garrard county, and nine years of the time I have been and am still a practising lawyer in said county. Dr. Evans during my acquaintance with him, has borne the character of a man of honesty and integrity equal to that of any man in the county, and I believe his statements are entitled to as much credit as any other man's. In this county he has borne the character of an honest, moral, upright man.

J. BURDETT.

Lancaster, Garrard County, Ky., May 4th, 1854.

I hereby certify that I have known Dr. Hezekiah Evans of this county for about twenty-five years. He is a gentlemen of undoubted veracity, and a man whose statement I would believe, either upon oath or in conversation, as soon as that of any other gentlemen of my acquaintance. My opportunities have

CERTIFICATES.

been very good to gain a knowledge of his character and standing, for I lived in his immediate neighborhood several years. I have been sheriff of this county for the last three years, and am still acting in that capacity.

J. A. BEASLY.

I, Paris Teeter, state that I am a minister of the gospel, and have been acquainted with Dr. H. Evans since his birth, and fully concur in the statements made by James A. Beasly given above.   P. TEETER.

I hereby state that I am a practising lawyer and have known Dr. H. Evans for ten or fifteen years, and concur in the statements made by James A. Beasly in regard to his character.   G. W. DUNLAP.

May 4th, 1854.

Lancaster, Garrard County, Ky., May 4th, 1854.

I, Edward Cooke, of the town of Lancaster and county of Garrard in the State of Kentucky, a native born citizen of said place, aged twenty-four years, and never resident elsewhere, do certify that so long as I have been acquainted with Dr. Hezekiah Evans, personally for many years and by reputation as long as my memory extends into the past, I have never heard aught said by friend or foe that would in the least tend to the disparagement of his character.

Just and upright in all his dealings with man, kind and generous, an unexceptionable companion in the family circle, he has made many friends who will cease to be so only in death.

As a physician I testify to the manliness and independence of his conduct. He would scorn to take advantage of any physician, how great soever his ignorance. I have been thrown into intimate relations with him as a physician, and have ever had pleasure in contemplating his truly gentlemanly deportment.

EDWARD COOKE, M. D.

Lancaster, May, 4th, 1854.

I do hereby certify that I have known Dr. Hezekiah Evans for the last thirty-five or forty years. He is a man of a resolute and determined character, and when he forms an opinion of men or things he is not easily changed therefrom. But I have always believed him to be honest and truthful, and believe that to be the opinion of those who are best acquainted with him. If I have heard his veracity or integrity questioned by any one, save by an enemy, it has escaped my recollection.   SAMUEL LUSK.

I am well acquainted with Samuel Lusk, and know that he was judge of the circuit court in this judicial district for several years. I have known Dr Hezekiah Evans for several years and fully concur in the opinion expressed of him in the above.   J W DISMUKES.

INTRODUCTORY SKETCHES;

THE COUNTRY.

The country occupied by the two parties is, geologically considered, of the transition formation, in which abounds the blue limestone of the Silurian system, of which Cincinnati is supposed to be the axis of upheaval. A little south of Lancaster may be found fragments of the old red sandstone, and perhaps of the sub-carboniferous rocks; but toward the river, the limestone appears in its full wealth. The scenery on Sugar creek is in many places truly beautiful and grand; and on the Kentucky river, the high perpendicular cliffs much resemble the sublime heights and palisades of the romantic Hudson. The soil is very fertile, as is its general character throughout Kentucky. The roads usually follow the meanderings of the creeks, to secure levelness.

Dr. Evans's residence is situated on a high hill, or rather, table land, while the houses of the Hills sit humbly in the valley. The accompanying map is not drawn with mathematical correctness, for it is designed to show merely the relative positions of the parties.

The people generally are moral, and well educated, and compose one of the best societies in the world. Their valor is world renowned, and one has only to visit them to have a heart throb with gratitude for unparalleled hospitality and kindness.

THE EVANS PARTY.

Gentle reader, permit me to give you a short sketch of the two belligerent parties.

The father of Dr. Evans was a native of Virginia. He moved to North Carolina while a young man, and married in 1788. He resided there about five years, then removed to Garrard county, Kentucky, and settled on Sugar creek, the theater of bloody tragedies, where he lived till his death, twenty-three years. He was blessed with twelve children, ten of whom he left living. He was truly a pious man, and a class leader in the Methodist church. The country being a comparative wilderness, and the people too few and scattered to build and support churches, his house was ever open to the worship of God, for he strictly taught his children the principles of the Bible, and there congregated his neighbors at the stated circuit preachings. These meetings often lasted several days, and to support them so frequently, kept him a poor man. He had plenty to be sure, but his surplus was thus devoted to religion.

Dr. Hezekiah Evans, the general of the Evans party, was born in 1801. At the age of fifteen, when his father died, he was left without a guardian, and little to be guardian for, save to support a widowed mother, and rear and educate four small children. These duties he faithfully performed, for they were the dying charges of his father. The old homestead of one hundred acres was left to his mother, which, at her death, was to be divided between the five younger sons. On this, his native place, the doctor worked very hard and supported himself and dependents in a laudable manner. He had no opportunity of educating himself, except the few minutes he employed in reading by hickory-bark fires before day light. In 1824 he married Miss Nancy Cole, of Indiana. He labored very hard on the little farm till 1829, when he was thrown from his horse and so badly crippled that he was unable to work for five years. During this confinement he studied medicine under a younger brother, and commenced the practice in his own neighborhood — without, however, charging fees for several years. Finally, for the support of his family, he was compelled to make charges for medical attendance ; but soon becoming dissatisfied with the profession, he discontinued it. But his neighbors, being so well pleased with him as a physician, entreated him to continue, which he did, and has since that time enjoyed a liberal practice.

The Evans party was composed of the Doctor, his five sons, and eight or ten other men. The majority of his sons were quite young, and could not well manage fire arms. The assistance received from abroad, was not particularly friendly to Dr. Evans, but at enmity with the opposite party. Four or five of the men, before the war, had been his bitter enemies, but their hatred for the Hills was still stronger ; and as the war assumed a general aspect, they united with the Doctor against the common enemy. Thus the Doctor did not know when to confide even in those fighting under his own standard. Had it been his desire, he could have secured the aid of his numerous relations, but he would not have them entangled in his reticulated contention — his motto being, " A few valiant hearts can withstand a host of the irresolute enemy ; and if we have to die, the fewer the better." Though they did not bear arms, we have reason to believe that they kept his treasury pretty well supplied.

The Doctor is a low, heavy set man, having all the characteristics of a genuine son of Erin. He is a fair specimen of durability, and looks as if he might have crossed the snowy Alps in one of Bonaparte's campaigns. From long and habitual watchfulness, his eyes wear a sleep-proof appearance, and his whole face looks defiance and presumptive *brass.* Phrenologically, combativeness is doubtless his most prominent trait, which, combined with a considerable quantity of genius, has given him his success in life. I spent nearly a week in his society, but, I must confess, I could not form much attachment for one so blunt and stern. I liked the boys very well, for they are agreeable and intelligent young fellows. And as for Mrs. Evans, there cannot be a finer and more clever lady.

The Evans party were vastly superior to their foes in point of intelligence, for the boys were pretty well educated, and the Doctor, besides his general information, seemed to understand the arts of war as taught in Scott's Tactics. Their arms consisted of about one hundred and twenty-five barrels of long and short arms (among which was numbered one of the famous Mississippi rifles), with bowie-knives in proportion. The rifle once belonged to the Hill party, but the Doctor knew it was too dangerous a weapon to stand before, and by using some of his cunning, obtained possession of it to do execution in his own cause.

THE HILL PARTY.

I am sorry that I cannot give so favorable a description of the Hill party as I did their foes — the one is to the other as day is to night.

Old John Hill, the progenitor of all the Hills, was a grand old knave and a *Tory.*

Jesse Hill, the father of Isaiah, Frederick, Russel, Jesse, Jr., and John, was an illiterate and dissipated man. He was drowned in Sugar creek while on a drunken spree. The whole band were mere tools used by certain politicians in elections to do their fighting and low dirty jobs. When they wanted a man "knocked down and dragged out," a point of the finger was all that was necessary.

In this manner they had whipped and driven off some fifteen good citizens before they got hold of Dr. Evans. They could whip a man, then "law" him for it and prove any thing they desired, so expert were they in the *art* of lying : and their relatives and friends were so numerous that they could not fail to have a superfluity of witnesses. Crowds of them would often go to elections and keep decent people away from the polls ; if they could not do it by other means, an abundance of rocks would do the work. Any land is truly unfortunate to be cursed with such a low, rowdyish clan.

I will here introduce another line of the Hill party. They, through pride, do not claim relationship with those above spoken of, but in reality some of them are as near as second or third cousins.

William Hill, the grandfather of Dr. Hill, was a drunken, dissipated old man.

John Hill, the Doctor's father, during the first part of his life, was as destitute of good character as any man could be. He married old Capt. Pollard's daughter — as fine a girl and as clever a woman as ever lived. She gave him all the enviable reputation he ever had, and a considerable amount of property. By these means he got to be constable awhile, and by management, intrigue, gambling, etc., he accumulated a little more property.

Dr. O. P. Hill's character was as bad as it could be till he married into the Salter family. He enjoyed a liberal education, but this was the more to the disadvantage of his neighbors, for his knowledge was employed to deceive them and breed discontent. After his marriage he got an extensive practice among his newly made relatives, and seemed to do well for a few years. But he was constitutionally so mean that he could not help falling back into his old dirty tricks, notwithstanding, on his mother's side, he had a numerous train of respectable connexions. All the respectable portion of his relatives were friendly to the Evans party, but all the ignorant, trifling and vagabond rabble were invariably their enemies. Dr. Hill was an extremely handsome man — tall, well proportioned, and very athletic.

The Hill party was comprised of near fifty men, supplied with as many arms as they could carry. They had force enough to demolish their enemies in a movement, but they were cowardly, and their leaders were as timid as school-girls. But nothing better could be expected of a people so ignorant and tutored in such dissolute habits. The majority of them spent their time in idleness, fishing, drinking, and gambling. They would idle away the week, or lie drunk in the most comfortable places, and when Sunday came, they would shoulder their fishing-poles, jugs of whisky, and decks of cards, and drive down to the creek to have a gambling and drinking frolic with the neighbors' negroes. They would first get them drunk and then cheat them out of their money, or steal it from them.

I will give you a specimen of their ignorance. Before the court, upon trial, one of the young stock, a lad of eighteen years, was asked, in substance, as follows : —

" Will you ever be punished if you swear a lie ? "

" Not as I knows on ! "

" Do you know how many months there are in a year ? "

" Don't know, sir; 'bout fifteen, I spose."

" How many days are there in a week ? "

" Don't know, sir."

" What month do you plant corn in ? "

" Don't know, sir ; reckon may be in January."

THE HILL AND EVANS FEUD.

THE ORIGIN OF THE FEUD.

CHAPTER I.

Dr. Evans hires a negro woman from John Hill — Hill induces her to run
away — Hill attacks the Doctor — The Law Suit — The Interview —
The Agreement.

OUR story, reader, like the monarch oak of the forest, that
disdains to bow to the tempest's wrath — like the mighty river
that pours its wealth of waters into the deep, has a small begin-
ning; and, like them, may not fill you with admiration at first,
but will elicit your attention as it grows in magnitude.

On the Christmas before Dr. Evans was crippled, in 1829,
he hired a negro woman from John Hill, the Doctor's father,
who was then acting as guardian for some orphan children.
During the following spring, John Hill concluded that he wanted
the negro's services himself, and thought of no better way of
securing them than by inducing her to run away from Dr. Evans.
Accordingly, he sent his niece, Hamilton Pollard's wife, on that
mission. The next morning the negro ran away and went to
Hamilton Pollard's house — Pollard went with her to Captain
John Hill's. The timid light of the new morn had scarcely
chased away the gloom of the night, when Mrs. Pollard went
to Swapshire's and told Mrs. Swapshire that the negro had run
away, and that Mr. Pollard had taken her to John Hill's. Mrs.
Evans, the old lady, happened to be at Swapshire's and heard
what was said, and told the Doctor, when she went home, which
was the first intimation he had of the negro's leaving. Dr.
Evans mounted his horse, with his crutches, being scarcely able
to ride, and went to see John Hill, and inquired if he had seen
the negro? Hill answered —

"I have not; nor do I know anything about her.'

"Did not Hamilton Pollard come here with her this morning? My mother told me he did."

"Yes—" replied Hill, hesitatingly, and feeling a little uncomfortable with a falsehood resting upon his tongue, "they came to my residence before I arose from the bed, and told me that she had run away. I told her to clear herself off, that I did n't want her about me."

"You have not treated me as a neighbor," replied the Doctor; "had a negro of yours run away and come to me, I would have secured and delivered her to you. But you did not choose to do so much for me. I will immediately prosecute Pollard for this *clever* trick."

Dr. Evans then turned and rode off about one hundred yards;—Hill called to him to stop.

"What evidence have you for the prosecution?"

"I have the evidence of my mother,—and if Mrs. Swapshire is a truthful woman, I will have the testimony to what your niece said."

"I would like to have the negro for the balance of the year," responded Hill. "I will charge you only for the time you have had her. If you keep the right of her services, she may put you to a great deal of trouble and expense."

"I hired her for the use of my family during the year, and intend to keep her;—and I will make those suffer who took her away."

The Doctor then rode off, and went to Swapshire's, not far distant. Mr. Swapshire told him all the particulars of the case. He then started to town to get out a warrant against Pollard. The road to town led directly by John Hill's blacksmith shop. As he approached the shop, he saw Hill and the negro standing in the yard.

"Where did you find her?" inquired the Doctor.

"After you left, I went out and called her—she came in and I brought her down here."

"What cause had she to run away?"

"She said she heard that you intended to whip her, and was afraid to stay on that account."

Dr. Evans told the negro to go home—at the same time giving her a tap on the head with his crutch. She started to ward home in a run, he following her. He had not gone more than ten or fifteen steps, when Hill ran up and struck him on the back of the head with a large hickory stick. He fell forward on the horse's neck senseless for a few moments, but remained in the saddle. When he recovered from the shock, he found that his horse had not moved, and saw Hill raising a heavy piece of iron to throw at him. He then observed:—

"John, you have done more than I ever expected you to do; you have sneaked up behind a crippled man and hit him. But you are too d — d a coward to look him in the face and strike!"

Hill raised the iron to throw. The Doctor slid down to the ground behind his horse. He was so weak that he had to lean on his horse's neck to support himself. Hill dropped the iron and ran to the house, it is presumed, to get his gun. The Doctor managed to mount again and went home. He had the wound on his head dressed, armed himself, and went back to the shop to cancel his account. Hill's partner was in the shop — he called for the account and paid it; then inquired where Hill had gone. He was informed that he had gone down to the mouth of Sugar-creek. As he rode back toward home, he saw Hill and Swapshire sitting near the road beside a tree. He exchanged salutations with Swapshire — then Hill spoke —

"How do you do?"

"None the better by you, you d — d old rascal!" was the surly reply.

Swapshire kept between them, and made apologies for what he had done. They both made apologies more than any *honest* men would — in the meantime slandering Mrs. Pollard, laying all the blame of the affair upon her. The Doctor, being very feeble, said but little, and passed on home. In a few days he brought a suit against Hill for damages, or, rather, for assault and battery. Of course Hill could have as many witnesses as he wished to call — those who would prove anything — hence, the Doctor only recovered one cent for a damaged head. Several months then passed away without any words between them. But during this time, Hill carried a heavy hickory stick; rumor said he intended to pay another cent for another damaged head. One day as he was going to Lancaster, Hill overtook and rode along behind him some distance. The Doctor drew his horse

2

to the side of the road to let him pass, and as he did so rode up beside him and said :—

"Report says you are carrying that stick for me — that you intend again to sneak up behind me. Now, take a little advice, and let me persuade you not to do so mean and dogged a trick. If you want to strike me, come up boldly like a man to my face and do it!"

"Sir, I have not carried this stick for you, nor have I intended to strike you again."

"If you should ever feel like it, it would do your soul good to try that stick upon me. Take my advice and do it speedily, for it will cost you nothing more than the trouble you will have in doing it."

"Then, sir, I extend to you the same liberty. If you should ever want anything out of me, it shall cost you nothing more than your trouble in getting it."

"Do you say that, sir! I could have it in my heart to give you a sound thrashing *now*, if I could do it in any way without putting my hands on your dirty, filthy person!"

"Well, you need not do it just now," replied Hill.

John Hill, I want to make an agreement with you. Have you enough native honesty about you to keep sacred your word of honor?"

"Make your proposition. Future deeds shall show my honesty."

"I want you to agree to let my business alone, if I will let yours alone."

"Let that, then, be agreed upon our honors."

In this manner they rode side by side some distance, and separated without blows or *very* aggravated words.

Thus, reader, you have the origin of a difficulty that has caused much blood to flow; which has thrown crowds of orphan children helpless upon the world; and filled the land with breathless anxiety. You have the first actions of the two parties. I leave it with you to decide who was the more to blame.

Dr. HILL AND THE LAW SUIT.

CHAPTER II.

Dr. Hill's Debut — Slander — The Law Suit — Dr. Hill as Witness — Perjured — Hills hired to whip Dr. Evans.

TIME rolled round several peaceful cycles, without any words between the two parties, till Dr. Hill began to practice medicine. Dr. Hill, notwithstanding the difficulty with his father, had hitherto professed perfect friendship for Dr. Evans. But this shallow and pretended friendship was doomed soon to have an end. Dr. Hill was attending on a sick lady by the name of Ellen Whicker. He had lost all hopes of her recovery, given her up to die, and told her friends that he could do nothing more for her. Dr. Evans was then called in to see the patient. The Doctor knew it was a delicate point to touch upon, and refused to go at first; but when he was sent for the fourth time, he went, not expecting to do any good more than the gratifying of her relatives. He examined the lady and found that she was curable. Under his prescription she soon got up and was able to go about. From that time forth, only enmity existed between the two Doctors. In a few days they met in the road — Dr. Evans gave the salute, but Dr. Hill refused to return it. This circumstance happened a second time, which was the first intimation that Dr. Evans had of the hostile state of feelings, without knowing the cause. Dr. Hill made it *convenient* to slander Dr. Evans on all occasions, calling him a d — d quack, and all other ugly names, and saying that he would kill every fever case that he chanced to be called to see. But actions always speak louder than words, and Dr. Hill, seeing his good success, could not refrain from saying, " He is a d — d lucky fellow ! " " What luck he has ! " " He never gets hold of any bad fever cases ! " These slanders became so multiplied and common that several of the neighbors informed Dr. Evans of them, and advised him to put a stop to them, even if he had to kill the perpetrator. The reply was, " Let him alone, he will soon kill himself. I care nothing about him, and will say nothing about him. He may yelp around as much as he pleases, so he keeps it out of my face."

Affairs continued thus some time, till one day when Dr. Evans went to Lancaster. He met there several of his professional brethren, but none of them deigned to speak to him. This was a mystery he could not solve. He was in town shortly after that, on one court day, when Mr. Quin, a man living in town, called him to see his sick children. He told Mr. Quin that he could not dare do such a thing in the midst of so many professional enemies — that they would whip him before he could leave town. But, finally, upon further entreaty, he went and saw the children. Dr. Hill saw this, which so infuriated him that he resolved to attack the bold foe who would thus dare to take a bone out of his lair. Dr. Evans returned to the court-yard, and was conversing with Col. Ray, when he heard some one behind him say —

"Sir, you have got to quit talking about me! I say, sir, a second time, you have got to quit talking about me!" (Dr. Evans turned round and saw Dr. Hill shaking a stick at him.) "You, sir, *you* — I say, sir, *you* have got to quit talking about me!" shouted Dr. Hill at the top of his voice.

"Me, sir?" replied Dr. Evans in a steady tone.

"Yes, you, sir!"

"I have not been talking about you; I never thought you worth talking about, nor no such a d — d puppy as you are. I have never said anything good, bad or indifferent about you — you are below the notice of any honorable man!"

"You *have* been talking about me and every physician in this town!" at the same time flourishing the large hickory stick over his head.

"You lie, sir; I have never talked about you or any other physician in this town! It does no good to be disputing in this manner; bring up your witnesses and prove what you say. It is a d — d lie, and you can't prove it, save by a low dog like yourself!"

Old man Baily stepped up to Dr. Evans and told him to go away — that he had said enough to satisfy every body about the slander.

"I'll cut your throat, sir!" shouted Dr. Hill, running his hand into his bosom.

This last tragi-comic display produced quite a sensation in the crowd, and an opening was made through which Dr. Evans slipped into the court-house. When he got to the door he observed, "You d—d scoundrel, you can't say that when you have not a gang of your *puppies* around to catch my arm!"

Here the quarrel ceased. The reader will perceive that the Hills were well trained to this kind of work ; — there were eight or ten of the young stock standing around, ready to seize Dr. Evans by the arms and disarm him if he had any weapons, then leave him to the merciless foe. Dr. Evans knew their plans of attack, and as he had no weapons, thought it best to make a safe retreat. Thus, it appears that Dr. Hill had been slandering Dr. Evans to the physicians of Lancaster, which explains their refusal to salute him. After this circumstance they treated him perfectly like a gentleman and friend.

The two Doctors had their next rencounter in 1840, when Dr. Hill appeared at court as a witness. Dr. Evans had brought a suit against the heirs of Major Burnsides for medical attendance. Through the instrumentality of the Hill and Salter families, the idea of a *steam-doctor* bringing a suit of *indebitatus assumpsit* on a medical account, produced quite a little excitement in the famous town of Lancaster. It made all the old revolutionary doctors wink and blink and shrug up their shoulders, while the young diploma-pill-bags ogled wisely and pulled down the corners of their mouths, as if to say, "*you can't come it, old fogy.*" The two *learned* lawyers employed on the opposite side, tried to *laugh* the case out of court — thus endeavoring to non-suit the Doctor. They are excusable for this ; for, when these precocious giants of the *green bag* get hold of a quick-sand case, upon which they can build no argument, they generally support their side by "laugh-and-grow-fat" ridicule. They tried another trick — argued that Dr. Evans was not a doctor because he had not a regular diploma, for which reason they argued also that his charges were illegal. But the court ruled out these schemes and proceeded to try the case according to its merits. The opposition then demanded a review of the Doctor's public and private life. His lawyers at first objected, saying —

" Who under heaven ever heard of a person's *private* character being brought into court for suing on an open account?"

But the Doctor told them to go ahead — that it was not money but character that he was contending for — that he would have cared little for the money, had they let his reputation alone. They then went into trial with the liberty of investigating his character to the utmost extent. The trial lasted two or three days. On the account the Doctor recovered $175, and a character worth more than gold — worth more than a whole El Dorado. Not a single black spot was proven in either his public or private life.

Dr. Hill stated to the court, in giving his *evidence*, that Dr. Evans had been attending a certain Mrs. Sherley, a sister of Dr. Dickerson, of Nicholasville — that she had gone deranged under his treatment, and that she had been taken to Mr. Welch's and cured by Dr. Dickerson. He was asked —

" Are you not mistaken? Did not Dr. Dickerson wait on her and pronounce her incurable? Was she not then carried to Mr. Swapshire's and cured by Dr. Evans?"

" I am not mistaken — there can be no mistake about it!" replied Dr. Hill.

" Did you not wait on a Miss Whicker and pronounce her incurable?"

" I did, and she died soon afterward."

" Did not Dr. Evans wait on her, and did she not recover under his treatment?"

" Positively not!"

" Did she not recover and bear two children?"

" She did not."

" Is it not possible that you are mistaken about this case?"

" I am *positive* — there is no mistake!"

Capt. James Murphy was then called to the bar and sworn. He stated that the lady did recover — that she lived some time after that and bore two children. Thus you see how nicely Dr. Hill was caught in a falsehood — and that, too, when he desired to blacken the character of another. Seeing himself thus caught in the intricate meshes of a lie, he went back to the court to explain, stating that Dr. Evans might have waited on her twice, or at another time. But Dr. Evans procured certificates from the lady's family and friends that he had attended on her only once, and that at the particular time mentioned.

To further stigmatize Dr. Hill, Dr. Evans intended to publish the evidence and facts of the case, but his friends persuaded him not to do so, that it would look more humane to show an enemy mercy. For the boldness of procuring these certificates, Dr. Hill sent him word that he intended to give him a certificate to h — ll. To which Dr. Evans replied, that he could not do it, for he was too base a coward — that he *might* get some of his loafers to do it — that if he had been aggrieved, he could get personal satisfaction any time. Thence forward Dr. Evans experienced a series of abuses from the lower class of the Hill party. It was soon known that Dr. Hill had hired a number of them at twelve and a half cents per day to whip Dr. Evans. They would often go up to him, curse and threaten him, in hopes of getting a fight. But Dr. Evans knew they were hired tools, and told them they had better work for their money in some other way ; that they could make more any other way than by whipping him. If I mistake not, one of the Hills upon his death-bed, told Dr. Evans that John Hill had offered ten dollars to any one who would whip him, and that he had attempted to get the prize money several times himself, but failed. And in his expiring breath begged pardon for throwing rocks at him on the public square in Lancaster. The Hills had a notorious fame for throwing rocks. Armed with these natural projectiles, they could do far more execution than with fire-arms — so truly and powerful where they hurled. A couple of them to go out on the hills squirrel hunting, would be more successful than as many good riflemen. They were extrémely afraid of Dr. Evans, for which reason their efforts at him were not so fortunate — but they had bravery enough to cast vagrant stones at his back.

While these troubles were in full blast, Dr. Evans chanced to meet John Hill on the creek one day ; and said : —

" Do you remember the agreement we made — that you

would let my business alone if I would do the same toward you ? I believe you are setting this gang of loafers on me. I *believe* it, and if I was certain of it, I would whip you right here like a dog ? But I do know one thing — they are your tools— you have perfect control over them, and if they trouble me any more I will hold you accountable for it. I will not act sneakingly about it as you do, but I will catch you in the court-yard, and give you as much of my stick as you are able to *pack* home. You can stop them and I know it — so look out for the future ! "

For some time after this incident, Dr. Evans had no more trouble — the Hills all seemed to be perfectly friendly with him.

THE BARBECUE FIGHT.

CHAPTER III.

The Election — Barbecue at Fred. Hill's — Dr. Evans drinks and treats — Stays till after dark — Hills get drunk — Dr. Evans informed of the plotted mob — He mounts his horse — Hills surround him — Jesse Hill strikes him — His horse knocked down — Confined in a corner — They shoot at the Doctor — The horse dashes out of their reach — They pursue — Dr. Evans escapes to Turner's — He arrives at home nearly dead — Random thoughts.

EVERY thing went on smoothly and peaceably between the two parties until the fall of 1849, at a barbecue given at Fred. Hill's. Here the war begins with more energy and on a larger scale. An election was soon to come off, if I am not mistaken, for delegates to the convention to revise the constitution of the State. There was considerable excitement — the emancipation question being warmly agitated.

Dr. Evans did not at first purpose to attend the barbecue, but after dinner having business in that direction, he concluded to stop a few minutes to see what was going on. He met Capt. Price, one of the candidates for the convention, who requested him to go to the barbecue and fill his place. The Doctor at first refused, but upon further entreaty told him he could not fill his place, but would do the best he could. He went, mingled with the heterogeneous crowd, and spent his money freely in *treats*. As the Doctor had not supped, the Hills' professing great friendship for him, urged him to stay and take supper with them. He stayed till after supper, and every thing went off so amicably that he did not even suspect an enemy on the ground. After supper he invited Richard Robinson to go home with him. A man by the name of Warren was standing near by and observed that he would like to go too, if they would wait for him awhile — that the *cream* of the barbecue had not come off yet. In a short time the Hill clan seemed to be getting a little too drunk, waving their hats and quarreling among themselves. These *signs* began to make the Doctor feel that all was not right. He observed to Robinson that nothing more could be effected for their party that night, and that it was time to be off. They started to get their horses — at which time the drunken, quarreling squad drew nearer and proposed to leave the decision of their dispute with Dr. Evans. He told them that he knew nothing about their contention, but that he would decide it in this manner—for them to say nothing more about it, and he would treat the crowd to a bowl of *mint sling*. He then walked to the bar (a low rail pen enclosing a barrel of whisky and the vender), and ordered it. While he was going up, one of the Hills patted him on the shoulder and said : — " Doctor, by G—d, you ought to treat ! " The Doctor immediately handed the bowl to him, but he turned and said, — " G—d d—m you, I would not drink to save your life ! " He then handed it to John Arnold, one of the candidates, and asked him to drink. Arnold took the bowl, immediately handed it to some one else, and asked him if he had a certain kind of medicine in his pill-bags. The Doctor said he had, and they started out to get it. They had gone only a few steps when John Murphy caught the Doctor by the arm, and said he wanted a word with him.

" You are out of the crowd now," said Murphy, " and don't go back into it again, for they are going to knock you in the head with rocks to-night ! "

" Who are ? "

" The Hills ! They have been following you around some time with their hands full of rocks ! "

" I reckon not ! "

" It is certainly true — don't you go back into the crowd any more. Have you any weapons to defend yourself with ? "

" I have none. Have you any to lend me ? "

" I have not," responded Murphy.

When the Doctor was called away, Jesse Hill took his place and walked off with Arnold to a large tree near by. The Doctor got the medicine and was returning to Arnold when he heard Jesse Hill remark : —

" I'll be d—d if I don't do it ! "

" I'd rather you would not," replied Arnold.

" I'll be G—d d—d if I don't ! " exclaimed Hill.

The Doctor then approached and said : — "Are you talking secrets, gentlemen ? "

" No, no ! " both replied, and Hill walked off to a group of his fellows, a few steps distant. " Here is the medicine, Mr. Arnold," observed the Doctor.

" I did not need the medicine — I merely wanted to get you out of the crowd, and tell you to get on your horse and leave immediately, for the Hills are going to mob you, and I don't want to see it."

The Doctor started to get his horse, which was hitched to the limb of a tree not far distant. As he pulled down the swinging limb to loose the bridle, he saw two men, supposed to be Bill Ware and Jesse Hill, follow him in a brisk gait and dart behind the tree. He thought they were trying to shoot and got behind his horse. They then turned and walked off rapidly toward the house. The Doctor mounted, rode out a few steps into open ground, found Warren there, and asked, " Are you ready to go ? "

" No ! " replied Warren. " Where is Robinson ? " " Gone to get his horse, I suppose ; get yours, and let us go — but stop, stay with me till he comes ; I am afraid to stay alone. I have learned that the Hills are going to mob me, and I don't want you to leave till Robinson comes ! "

Warren walked immediately off without saying a word, and was seen no more that night. Bill Ware who was a perfect stranger to the Doctor, then went up and spoke :

" Are you going home to-night ? "

" Yes, sir, I am," replied the Doctor.

" Hold down your head," said Ware, taking hold of his hand, " I want a word with you. I understand that you intend to knock me in the head with rocks to-night."

" Good Lord ! " exclaimed the Doctor, " who could have told that lie ! "

As these last words were falling from the Doctor's lips, Jesse Hill struck him on the side of the head with a square bar of iron. He snatched his hand away from Ware, and asked —

" Who is that throwing rocks at me ? "

" No body," replied Ware.

" Some one hit me, and there's the man ! " — pointing to

Jesse Hill, who was standing in a throwing position not far distant, in the direction the blow came from.

"I did'nt do it, sir," responded Hill.

"I think you did Jesse, and I would like to know what you did it for!"

" Upon my honor I did not throw. I have nothing against you, and I did not throw ; but I *can* do it if you want me to!"

"I don't want you to do it, Jesse!"

" By G—d, we'll give you a *few* any how!" exclaimed Hill.

During this conversation, the Doctor cast his eyes around to see who was near, and the best way to get out. He saw not less than twenty-five of the party surrounding him, and advancing in platoon order, so as to form a hollow-square. When Hill said " we'll give you a few any how," the Doctor wheeled his horse and sprang him toward a gap in the fence. As he did this, the rocks began to fly. His horse ran about ten steps and was knocked down. About the time the horse fell, the stones knocked the Doctor perfectly blind ; though he retained his seat—and indeed it was impossible for him to fall, for the rocks came as thick and fast as hailstones. When one would knock him in one direction, another would knock him as far the other way, in such a manner as to keep him vibrating like a pendulum. They ran the horse up between the tobacco-house and fence, and having them thus confined, beat both horse and rider nearly to death with rocks, rails, boards, and poles. The Doctor, though yet blind, besought them to have mercy on him — but the more he begged, the harder and faster the pelting missiles flew. The horse finally got out; but how he did it, is a mystery, for the fence was close to the house and very high, and strongly *staked* and *ridered*, while behind, the enraged mob stood as thick as forest trees. When the horse got out and had gone about half round the house, the Doctor's eyesight returned. He still clung to his saddle, though the shower of pelting stones did not abate its fury. When the horse got back to the place from which he started, the Hills shot at the Doctor twice, with a small and a large pistol. The horse being easily frightened, scared at the report and dashed away beyond the reach of the stones. As the pistols were fired, one of the formest of the pursuing party fell over a stump, and nearly all the rest stopped to seize their supposed victim, while the Doctor made good his retreat under the cover of night. Those who continued the pursuit turned to the left to intercept him in the road which led to his house ; but instead of taking the road, he turned to the right through the woods. He had not gone more than fifty yards before he fell from his horse : but this did not stop him, for he ran on his hands and feet, alternately rising and falling, till one of his sons found him, and aided him to mount. The Doctor was nearly senseless, and called loudly for water. But the son knew it would not be expedient to delay a moment, and ordered his father to follow him.

" Ride faster father, they might overtake us !" said the son, as he heard the drunken rabble in their noisy pursuit.

" Oh son ! I can't do it—I am almost dead !"

" Good Lord !" exclaimed the son, " what shall we do ; yonder they are ahead of us again in the main road ! We must take the other end of the road and out-run them, for we can't out-fight them !"

" Let us gallop on son ; throw down the fence and go the nearest way to Bill Turner's house, for if I don't get some water soon, I can't live."

They went on about half a mile to Turner's, and called for water. The Doctor asked Turner :

" Have you a gun ?"

" I have a rifle !" replied Turner.

" Is it a sure fire ?"

" Not very."

"I want it anyhow, if it will shoot at all; will you load it for me?"

" Yes ; but won't you get down and stay awhile ?"

"I believe I will, for I would like to wash my wounds in whisky, if you have any. Then I must go back after my hat and saddlebags. I find my wounds to be so bad that if I remain long they will get sore, and I will not be able to get away."

" You are unable now to get home ; you had better stay here," replied Turner.

"I will try it anyhow, if you will go with us and lend my son your gun."

" I will give you all the assistance in my power."

After the Doctor washed his wounds in whisky, they set out and arrived at home without further disturbance. The Doctor was bruised perfectly black nearly all over, and his chest was very much swollen. His jaw-bone was broken in two places, and his head had not a few gashes. These wounds and bruises kept him in bed nearly two months, and so severe were they, that the neighbors dispaired of his recovery.

I have no feelings of enmity for the Doctor, but I could have it in my heart to rejoice that this misfortune befell him, for he certainly deserved a *sound thrashing* for being caught at such a place at so late an hour. The Doctor claims to be a respectable man, which claim I do not in the least doubt, but this would seem to indicate that his code of morals, or standard of respectability was not very elevated, and may perhaps make some people skeptical as to the justness of his pretensions. It is true that *honorable* men do sometimes visit such gatherings, but a man of high-toned refinement would not be seen there, unless he chanced to be a candidate. But how can we justify a man, pretending to *any* respectability in society, in mingling and drinking with such a motley, ruffian crowd, at so late an hour ? I am persuaded that the Doctor had imbibed too freely of the *ardent*, for if his soul was not drunk, it was certainly devoid of sensibility. Every departure from nature's laws brings its penalty, and severe the penalty proved in this case to him. Of all the despicable evils, that of being thrown into a ruffian crowd, stirs up the most bitter disgust and horror in my soul. And had the Doctor any moral sensibility, or any feelings of native pride, he would have felt this same detestation and bitterness of heart for those with whom he mingled.

I am utterly opposed to those debasing assemblages on election occasions ; they do no good, but inestimable evil. They are given by the parties—not so much to hear political discussions as to gain friends and secure votes by the magnificence and *magnanimity* of their TREATS. This custom has grown upon the people to such an extent that the man who can *treat* the most, drink the most " LIKER" and make himself the *bigest* fool while drunk, is almost certain to be elected. This is a lamentable fact. In many instances have worthless topers been preferred to men of talent and morality. Now, if I could not be elected but by these drunken *beasts*, I would disdain the honor, stamp it under foot as I would the necks of the senseless vagabonds that gave it. Such drunken honors I would cast to the swine, as unworthy a man possessed of a soul.

This liquor-bribery custom not only debauches men, but leads directly to another evil even more lamentable to an American—that of SELLING VOTES. It cannot be denied that some of the chivalric sons of old Kentucky are becoming so debased as to sell their votes with impunity. Had I an ocean of tears to weep for their depravity! I never even thought of such a thing as selling votes; selling the liberties of freemen, the franchise of the ballot-box, till I visited the hills of my childhood, in Garrard county. What superlative disgust stirred the inmost cells of my heart on learning that some of my native county-men were thus dead to the noble and elevated principles of our glorious liberty! These are hard words for the county of my nativity, but mild in comparison to the indignation aroused by such heathen degeneracy. This cannot apply to the people generally, for Garrard county boasts of some of the most noble and patriotic men that breathe American air, and I love her for her greatness; but every flock has its black sheep.

I am no temperance advocate myself, nor particularly in favor of Maine-liquor-law-like statutes, but it does seem that it would be a blessing to the State, and to the whole Union, for the legislature to enact measures to prevent this corruption in elections. No penalty could be too severe for the low miscreant who would sell his vote, or the vile-hearted wretch who would buy it. For, let the evil go unchecked, and what would be the result? The base scoundrel who had the most money would be sure of election. Then see what a condition our country would be in. The men of intelligence and moral worth would disdain to contend for such degraded honors, and our legislative halls would be filled with all the vice and depravity of the land. Such *guardian angels* of our liberties would soon demolish the towering temple of freedom, humble her proud columns to the dust, and shut the world in darkness. We could but weep over her beautiful and classic ruins.

We see Dr. Evans countenancing and participating in a vice

that leads directly to this dire fate. One vice leads to another. But he has dearly paid for his erring ways, and can repent at leisure, and I am confident that he will not be guilty of the like again. I could wish that the same punishment were visited upon every perverse Kentuckian who has strayed into these dismal paths of corruption. This is hard reproof for my countrymen, but they must pardon me for daring to speak so boldly the sentiments of a heart that received its first impulses in the generous and patriotic community of their glorious State.

HILLS LURK AROUND DR. EVANS'S HOUSE.

CHAPTER IV.

False rumors — Mrs. Rus Hill's debut — Woman's depravity — Jesse Hill's chase — Bravery of the little boys — Hill's horses found in the Doctor's orchard — Two of the boys retreat before a party of the Hills — Neighbors help the Doctor to defend his house — Squire Level and Ben Dunn take the horses.

THE barbecue fight happened on Saturday evening, and on the Monday following, it was rumored by the Hill party that the Doctor had been seen lurking near one of their houses. This was entirely false, for he was scarcely able to move a limb, from the soreness of his wounds.

Time, pregnant with dire events and livid crimes, soon raised the curtain and exposed Mrs. Rus Hill to the scorn of the expectant multitude. The sinking sun shone forth in all the resplendency of his evening glory, but mantled in a mournful blush of crimson, that youthful innocence had thus grown to aged depravity. She took her child into her arms, and with the *sincere* affectation of an expert actress, set out from her lone cabin of rudeness, and made the welkin ring with lamentations for her miserable fate. The proud hills, disdaining to listen to such airy wailings, repulsed the empty sounds and with reproof echoed them from their rock-ribbed sides to the ear of their degenerate mistress; — while the crystal waters murmured along their innocent way, leaping with joy and child-like gambol, apparently unconscious that one so repulsively black with crime was mirrored on their bright surface. But she bellowed most lustily and made the big tears stream like liquid diamonds down the furrows of her woe-begone countenance, to attract the attention and commiseration of the passer-by; and well did she succeed, for Mr. Gardner, James Hutson, and William Walls, ever tender to the woes of others, inquired into the cause of her overflowing grief.

"I'm 'fraid to stay at home," bellowed she; — "Dr. Evans has been shooting at me all day. He stands behind the big

3

beech tree and shoots into the door. Two of the balls struck the cradle in which my child was sleeping. I picked up the balls as they rolled across the floor, for here they are now." (She held out to exhibition two balls that had never been in a gun.) " Being very much alarmed for the safety of my child, I took it up in my arms and walked to the door; he shot at me again and struck the door-facing. I then started to run through the corn, the negro woman bringing the other children, and he shot at me twice again, cutting the corn blades near me."

Reader, this incident will give you an inkling of the depth in degradation to which some women are capable of descending. Were this the extent of her depravity, I could rejoice; but it is an episode to the gloomy scenes yet to be revealed by our history. It does seem that woman is susceptible of an infinite degree of either virtue or vice. A maiden, just blooming into maturity, may possess a purity of heart and holiness of mind that elevates her to a comparative level with the chanting seraphs of angelic glory — then again, her heart may be full of the blackest vice, and her mind such a demoniac work-shop as to merit the lowest pit in the infernal regions. The one, we can but admire and love, the other, despise and abhor. See this woman as she walks down the creek, *bawling* deception, with her little *innocent* in her arms. What a contrast! Her bosom is stained with all the vice to which human beings are heir, while the cheerful babe, innocence and purity personified, peeps forth with its bright little eyes upon the beauties of nature, a stranger to guile, and unconscious of the boisterous passions and rankling depravity of the one in whose arms it rests.

After she had gone, Walls told his comrades that her tale was all a lie, for he had been to Dr. Evans's during the day, and he was unable to get out of the house. Further down the creek, she met David Gordon, and told him the same *yarn*. He invited her to go home with him, but she refused, and went on down the creek, making the woodland slopes reverberate with her lamentations. The next morning, Gordon went down to Rus Hills's, and saw where some one had actually shot the door-facings. But we have reason to believe that the Hills did the shooting themselves, in order to raise the report, and have the *signs* for evidence. After widely circulating this report, and exulting in their success, they determined to swear out a warrant against the Doctor. But James Naler, John Hill's nephew, told them they could not prove anything against him, for his uncle, and aunt, and Mrs. Hutson, had been staying at Dr. Evans's house all day, expecting him to die of his wounds. With this counter evidence, they said nothing more about it till the sitting of the grand jury, when they attempted to bring it up ; but the jury would pay no attention to them. Thus ends a tale of female baseness, a baseness too enormous, I hope, to find room in any other woman's heart.

The object of the Hills in spreading these reports was to get public sentiment in their favor, and make it appear justifiable in the eyes of the world for them to beset Dr. Evans's house. Circumstances soon proved that they had succeeded in their design. One morning the Doctor sent out one of his little sons to the pasture to get a horse to go to mill. He came running back, very much alarmed, without the horses, and said Jesse Hill was out there. The Doctor, though scarcely able to walk, took up an old rifle and a small pistol and started to rout him. He told some of the little boys to bring the ammunition, and tried to make the others stay ; but they would not—one of them, Sam, led the way. They went to the place where Hill had been seen ; but he was then invisible. They believed him to be hid somewhere near, and began to search. Soon, the little fellow who had the pistol, jumped him up behind a bank of earth, and ran after him with all his might, without ever thinking of his pistol, and hallooing : " Yonder he is—yonder he is ! shoot him, Pap — shoot him, Pap ! " As Hill ran off about one hundred and twenty yards distant the Doctor fired, but missed him. The little boys ran on in pursuit, presenting a miniature buck chase. The Doctor found a horse belonging to one of the Hills hitched in his pasture. He turned it into Hill's field, and called to the boys to know where they were. To this call, two of the Hills, lower down in the thicket, near their own house, answered :

" Here we are, G — d d — n you ! Go and get those other horses and turn them through also, you d — d old rascal ! "

" Are they your horses, Rus ? " replied the Doctor. " If they are, you had better come and get them."

" Turn them through, you grand old scamp, or you 'll be responsible for them. If you don 't, we 'll *get* you."

" You had me once, but did n't kill me ; — but I don 't thank you for not doing it ! If you want me, here I am — come and get me — I am at the service of even such poor, pitiful scoundrels as you are ! "

On his return home, the Doctor found three other horses hitched in the orchard, but did not know to whom they belonged. He started two of his sons to mill, the remainder to school. The two going to mill had gone about half a mile to the creek, when a party of the Hills gave chase and ran them back home. In the meantime the Doctor sent a negro boy to one of their houses to inform them that they could get their horses. On receiving intelligence of this fact, they replied that they were d — d sorry that they were absent, for they would have taken out the black scoundrel's heart. The Doctor then sent the boys around to several respectable neighbors to invite them to come with their guns and help defend the house, or give counsel for future actions. They came and saw where eight or ten horses had been hitched around the fence, beside those in the orchard, with signs indicating that they had been standing there all night. They knew not what advice to give, but two or three of them, whom the Hills had mutilated almost as badly as they had the Doctor, remained with their rifles. Before night, about twenty of the Hill party collected on the creek, and swore they would have their horses that night or die, and if the *old coon* did not keep a sharp look out, they would take the white house. Late in the evening Col. Hall Anderson saw the party and advised the Doctor of the danger, and also informed him that one of the horses belonged to the wife of old Henry Ware, and the others to John Hill, jr., who had nothing to do with the difficulty. John Hill, jr., had sent them down to old John Hill's in a wagon loaded with lumber, and through Mr. Anderson asked if he could get them. The Doctor replied —

" He can come unarmed ; I have no objection to his coming in daylight, but as it will be dark before he can get here, I rather he would wait till morning. I will have his horses stabled and well attended to."

The Doctor then posted six sentinels around the house, with

orders to shoot *everything* that came near enough.   Four guns were heard during the night, but no one was found hurt in the morning.   He sent a note to John Hill, informing him that he could get his horses in perfect safety — that no one would be allowed to hurt him.   Hill replied that he knew the Doctor would not molest him, or permit it to be done if he could help it; but, as Sellars was there, he feared to go.   'Squire Level, seeing so much preparation on the previous evening, supposed they had an action, and came up to learn who had fallen on the battle field.   The Hills had previously sent for Ben. Dunn. As these gentlemen were particular friends of the Doctor, the Hills requested them to go and bring the horses.   When they went up to the Doctor's house, they informed him that there was no crowd of Hills collected below — the only persons having been seen were old John Hill, *little* John Hill, and Col. Hall Anderson.   But the Doctor knew better the tricks of the party, and told them if they wanted to see a crowd lying in ambush, all they had to do was to look into the bushes as they returned. And, sure enough, they did see some fifteen or twenty, with their rifles, lying in the shade.   They delivered the horses and left as quickly as possible.   From that time forth the Hills continually lurked around the house and shot at any of the family who chanced to be seen.

I do not know that I ever heard of the stern and rigid laws of our enlightened State being violated with such impunity.   They roved, a bandit clan, insulting and stamping bleeding justice to the earth.   The whole country should have arisen in arms and humbled in the dust the necks of the miscreants who would thus dare to violate the laws.

SUNDRY INCIDENTS.

CHAPTER V.

THE next incident happened on the creek. The Doctor's
negroes and sons were pulling fodder in a little field near the
creek, and to see how they were progressing, the Doctor
shouldered his rifle and went down there. He soon heard a
wagon coming up the road, and saw that Rus Hill was driving
it. As soon as Hill saw him, he began to rip out some of the
blackest blasphemies, and stopped his wagon about thirty paces
distant.

"You d—d old rascal, what are you doing? You had better go away from there!" said Hill.

The Doctor said not a word, but very leisurely laid his gun
on the fence, as if to shoot.

"Oh, don't shoot — don't shoot — you are mistaken, it was
not me, it was not me — I had no hand in it!" imploringly
cried Hill.

"You are a liar, Sir! I am not mistaken; defend yourself
or die!" replied the Doctor.

The Doctor leveled his gun and took deliberate aim at Hill's
breast, but the cap snapped. He put on a second and a third
cap, but all missed fire. During this time, Hill was standing
before the oxen, fair to view; but when the fourth cap went
on, he ran behind the wagon, drew a large pistol, and presented
it as if he intended to shoot.

"Shoot, you cowardly puppy!" said the Doctor.

Hill raved and cursed desperately, making so much noise
that the boys came from the corn-field to assist their father.

" Shoot the dirty scoundrel, and don't let him curse you that way ! " exclaimed the boys.

" Go back to the pulling of your fodder; his words are nothing, I can manage him ! " replied the Doctor, calmly.

" Fetch them all out,— sons, negroes, women, children and all — I can whip the whole camp-meeting of you ! " shouted Hill, flourishing his pistol over his head, to indicate his boisterous bravery.

Nancy Baker, one of his *particular* friends, went to him. They talked awhile in a low voice ; then she went to the Doctor.

" Get over the fence and fight him a fair fight ! " said she.

" Madam, I am not able to fight any one ; and as you are one of his *good* friends, you had better stay with him."

" Go away then, and let him pass."

" I have a right to my own fence, and I will stay here, at least, till I get rested."

Mr. Naler then came along, and said he was afraid to pass while two such belligerent fellows were near; and that he might pass safely, asked the Doctor to go away. The Doctor did as requested. Naler drove the wagon past; while Hill walked beside it, to shelter himself, even after the Doctor had gone away two or three hundred yards distant.

These snappings made the Doctor believe that he should not take revenge for past injuries ; and from that time forth he only acted on the defensive, up to a certain period. This opinion betrays a good deal of superstition. It reminds me of old lady who would not flog her son because the first lick broke the switch, believing it to be the decree of heaven thus manifested, that she should not whip him. This was a dangerous policy for him ; he would not take the proffered advantage of the law, which rendered his arms inoffensive. Had he shouldered his rifle, searched the country, and shot down every Hill that he chanced to meet, the law could not have hurt him, since they had threatened and already attempted his life ; and this, too, would have brought the war to a speedy close.

The Doctor soon got out a peace warrant against the Hills. But the constable could not, or would not, serve it on more than two or three of them. This was a desperate state of affairs ; —

the law had no power, and the Hills bid audacious defiance to all opposition.

In the mean time, the Hills, with shouldered rifles, scoured the country, swearing they would serve a *peace warrant* on the *old white headed coon* at the first opportunity. They continually laid around the house and shot at every one seen, either black or white. One evening when the front door was half open, one of the boys passed by it, going up stairs; at that instant an ounce ball was fired at him. It passed through the side light of the door, and had it not been for the half of the door which swung open, it would have killed him. The ball glanced from the swinging door and fell at his feet on the stair-way. Many such incidents might be pointed out, but this one is sufficient to show the eminent danger to which Dr. Evans and his family were continually exposed. The reports and long echoes of guns were so many familiar tunes, and the rattling balls on the house top lively accompaniments to the music. They had the house perfectly besieged — every road and outlet had its blockade of *veteran* troops. Of course the Doctor and his family had to keep pretty close and quiet, through motives of personal safety. Jesse and William Hill had command of the forces employed in this siege, which lasted more than two months.

About the first of March, the Doctor was called to see a patient in the family of Ben. Dunn, who resided just across the creek. On the way thither, he had to pass the house of old John Hill, who professed to have nothing to do with the difficulty. He knew the Doctor's destination, and immediately sent a negro messenger with the news to Rus Hill. Rus came, and as the Doctor returned, went to the door and tried to shoot, but his gun would not fire. The Doctor jerked a pistol from his holster, Hill jumped back, and he rode on unhurt. From this you may see their mode of operation. Old John Hill professed perfect friendship for the Doctor, but in reality was the general of the Hill party. He would not come out boldly before the enemy, but staid in the back ground and *boldly* gave orders for others to *boldly* fight by. After this incident, he went another way to Mr. Dunn's, but they soon discovered that trail and waylaid him, though it was through open ground and they could not lie in ambush. On one occasion they besieged the Doctor at **Mr.**

Dunn's house, and kept him there nearly a week, and that too, within a short mile of home. Finally, during a very dark night, he succeeded in making a safe retreat. A man could scarcely be hunted more perseveringly, or watched more closely than the Doctor was. Of course he had to use considerable cunning and dexterity to keep out of their clutches. But if he saw a party in open ground, and started toward them, they would turn upon their heels and make tracks in double quick time.

The Doctor wished to sow a piece of oats, but feared to let the boys do it, for the field was surrounded on three sides by a continuous thicket. But they told him that there was no danger of the Hills molesting them if he would give them his *old hat*. The Doctor thought this rather a strange idea, but obeyed their request. The field was in sight of Rus and Bill Hill's houses. The boys took the old hat and placed it nearly behind a tree, so that it looked like the Doctor standing guard, and peeping round the tree to watch the Hills. Every night they changed the position of the hat, as if the *wearer* had changed to a more comfortable posture. The Hills thought it was the veritable Doctor himself standing guard. They continually shot at it with their ounce balls, and cursed it with the most bitter oaths, telling it to " come down here, you old bald headed coon, and get something to drink, I know you are *dry* — there's nothing like having plenty of " *liker*" to drink and a good horse to shoot from! " After these eloquent harangues, they would mount their horses, gallop around a tree and shoot at it, to show the Doctor's *old hat* what good marksmen they were, and how well their horses were trained. Thus, even an old hat was as much guard as needed, until the boys finished sowing their oats. The Doctor's hat must have imbibed some of the *military* from his warlike head ; at any rate, *it knew how to stand guard pretty well.*

The Hills drew many other people, and even strangers, into their difficulty. They gave little dancing parties, wood-cuttings, log-rollings, house-raisings, etc., to collect crowds of the floating loafers of the country. When thus collected, they pleasantly detained them with the fiddle's charm, and the bold spirit of Bacchus, and with the embraces of women of no enviable reputation. What could better please a rabble crowd — frolic, whisky and women! These were the tools needed to help prosecute the war, for no respectable person could be caught in such society, or voluntarily engage in such a disastrous strife. You may know that even the females of the Hill party had no exalted opinion of virtue, when such names as *Sall Hill's Bill*, etc., are familiar to the citizens of Garrard; no better name having been found for a numerous class of progeny whose paternal origin is debateable

THE COURT-HOUSE TRAGEDY.

CHAPTER VI.

In March, 1850, the Doctor went to Lancaster to attend
court. Two of his sons accompanied him, one about eighteen,
and the other about fourteen years of age. As none of the
Hill party made their appearance, and as Judge Robinson was
expected to deliver a political speech in the evening, they
concluded to remain till that time. During the speech, the
Doctor, however, took the precaution of posting his sons on
guard in the rear, so that none of the party could creep up
unperceived. The Judge had not spoken many minutes, when
half a dozen Hills were seen in the aisle, holding a council of
war. The Doctor watched them narrowly, and soon saw that
he would have to fight his way out, if he got out at all ; for
they had formed nearly an entire circle around him. It was
very evident from their *moves*, that Bill Ware had been chosen
to do the shooting. He attempted to shoot several times, but
as soon as the Doctor threw his piercing glance at him, he
would turn and walk out of the door. At the opposite door
there was another party, with Jesse Hill at their head — but
they were closely watched by the boys. Jesse attempted to
shoot, and even presented his pistol once, but at the same

instant seeing the boys with their dreaded pieces coming down on him, dropped it and walked out of the house. He then went over to the tavern, took a glass of brandy, flourished his pistol in the air, and swore he would never take another drink of liquor till he had killed the Doctor or one of his sons. He returned to the court-yard, dashed around in a wild frenzy, and insulted several people ; and even hawked and spat in the face of one Mr. Dollings, cursed him, and told him to take THAT, if he did not he could get THIS, at the same time shaking the pistol over his head. Dollings walked immediately away.

Alexander Arnold then went into the house and said to Dr. Evans : —

"Jesse Hill is out there *ranting* around ; your little son is out there also. You had better go out and take care of him, he might get killed."

The Doctor not being very well acquainted with Arnold, thought it might be a trick of the party to get him out, and replied : —

"He is smart enough to take care of himself in any crowd, how small soever he may be."

"I thought it my duty to inform you of the fact; his danger certainly demands attention," replied Arnold.

"I am much obliged to you, sir, for the information—accept my thanks."

At this moment, a crowd with great excitement, came rushing in at the door, some crying "let me get away, for God's sake let me get away." The Doctor pushed his way through the crowd to the door, and saw one of his sons standing near the door, the other on the steps of the court-yard enclosure, both with their hands in their pockets on their pistols, while their pale countenances trembled with excitement. Their anxious eyes directed him to the danger. He saw James Ward in the corner of the yard trying to pull Jesse Hill away — Jesse struggling violently to free himself. As soon as Hill saw the Doctor, he cursed Ward, and gave him to understand that more *persuasive* means would be used, if *words* could not obtain his freedom. He struggled desperately, and shook off his best friend. Ward walked away behind the corner of the court house. The Doctor stepped back against the door-facing, ready to draw his cocked pistols. Hill walked directly toward him, and drew his revolver. The Doctor making a gesture, said:—

" Jesse, you had better go away."

" G—d d—n you," said Hill, making vague gestures, " come on, I am not afraid of all HELL."

" You had *better* go away," said the Doctor with more emphasis.

Hill advanced to within ten or fifteen feet, turned his right side to the Doctor, threw up his pistol and exclaimed —

" G—d d—n you, *now crack your dasher*."

As he uttered these words, and was bringing down his pistol, the Doctor drew his instantly and shot him under the arm. When the smoke of his pistol blew away, the Doctor saw him aiming and pulling at the trigger of his pistol. He stepped two steps forward, which threw him behind the other facing of the door. A voice was heard from the crowd, " Doctor, you hav'nt touched him! " He stepped back to his former position, saw Hill leaning against the court-house with his revolver in both hands trying to shoot the boy on the enclosure steps. The Doctor again raised and fired, and shot him through the heart. When the ball struck him, he sprang half bent and fell about five feet from the court-house. Thence he sprang twelve or fifteen feet and fell on the right side of his head. As he was thus turning a summerset in the air, the Doctor fired again, but missed. The same unknown voice from the crowd exclaimed — " Don't shoot any more, Doctor, you have killed him." He retained his position some time, expecting every moment that Ware and a half dozen more would be shooting at him. When the curious crowd formed a circle around Hill, the Doctor stepped up a few benches and watched their movements through the window. That was the safest place to be found, for no one could sneak up behind him, and he had full view of both doors. When the fight began, the house was perfectly crowded; but when it ended, the Doctor was the lone occupant. The people disliked to see these actions between the two parties, for they feared to be brought into court as witnesses, for they might thereby render themselves liable to incur the displeasure and malice of one of the parties, and peradventure by this means

be thrown into the maelstrom of the war. It is not certain that
Hill fired at all, but *Madame Rumor* say he did. The boys
soon went in.

"Father, we had better leave here and go home!"

"I will not go — I've done nothing to go for, and do not
intend to go," replied the Doctor, in a petulant tone.

"Oh, *father*, *please* come on; we will all be killed in here
if we stay — this is no place for us now, and we had better get
away!"

The Doctor then went out at the door, where he expected to
find Ware with his hostile clan, and walked across the square,
with pistol in hand, to where his horse was hitched. A friend
ran up to unhitch his horse for him, but the Doctor pushed him
away and said: —

"I want neither friend nor foe to lay hands on me!"

About that time some one, supposed to be the sheriff, jumped
upon the court-yard steps, and hallooed —

"Catch him, catch him — don't allow a man to shoot another
down in the *court-yard* and *then* get away! I command the
mule-ishe (militia) to take him!"

This was evidently a fellow of *corpulent* words and *lean*
actions, a specimen of the *genus homo* that the Young America
spirit of the age calls "*gas*." When the Doctor heard this
pompous harangue, he left his horse, advanced to within fifteen
steps of *the* orator and the crowd, and said: —

"Gentlemen, if any of you feel like it, come out and try
your hand, try the virtues of lead! Choose your champions, or
all come together — I am ready for any emergency, life or
death!"

A friend brought his horse and urged him to go; the boys,
likewise, still entreating him to leave. He then told the younger
son to get his horse and saddle bags in order to leave. The boy
did as directed, and they galloped across the square past the
crowd. The other son had not yet mounted. As they were
passing they encountered a shower of rocks from men not, till
then, supposed to have any *interest* in the affair. The whole
crowd ran in pursuit, yelling like Indians; some mounted horses
and with pistols in hand, set out in full speed. The older boy,
Sam, I believe, soon mounted, and with a fleet horse got before

the pursuers. When he passed the foremost one, who was Elijah Duggins, he wheeled his horse and observed —

" You dirty puppy, this shows where you stand ; — come another step and I will shoot you down ! "

Sam stood there with his pistol presented ; the crowd wheeled and ran back about as fast as they came. These were the *brave mule-ishe* so *bravely* commanded and so heroically repulsed by a beardless youth. Kentucky is renowned for her Spartan bravery, but little valor could be anticipated in such a rabble crowd as this. The flying party then rode on without further molestation.

When he reached home, the Doctor appeared a little excited, and his wife asked —

" What is the matter, dear ? "

" Oh, nothing, only I have killed Jesse Hill ! "

" How do you know you have killed him ? "

" I *know it*, because I saw him die."

" Where did you hit him ? " inquired she, seeming considerably excited.

" I did not miss his right nipple more than half an inch. But pray, tell me, are you going to give me anything to eat ? "

" Good Lord ! you don 't want to eat ! "

" Yes I do ; I 'm very hungry. Make haste ; the whole party will be here on me in less than half an hour. I want to eat to be strong enough to whip the whole crowd, and I fear I shall not have time to do it."

He immediately dispatched a negro to the fields to tell the other boys and William Chrismon to come in with their guns and prepare for a general battle. Just as the Doctor finished his dinner, he saw the sheriff, his deputy, and four other men approaching. Some of these were his friends. It was reported that a mob, about fifty strong, had stopped a few hundred yards distant, between the house and the creek. When the sheriff and party rode up, the Doctor, through his sons, told them —

" Gentlemen, you must not come in here."

" Ask your father how many times he shot," replied the sheriff.

" He shot three times."

" If he did, tell him to not let it be known ; for it is rumored in town that there were only two shots, and they were so close together that one man could not have shot them both. The people generally believe that he and Jesse Hill shot about the same time. Tell him to let the report go that way, for it would be more favorable for him."

" He does not desire any such report, for it is untrue, and he wishes only the truth to go to the world. He did actually shoot three times, for it took that many loads to *fill up*."

" Tell your father he had better surrender himself to me ; it will be better for him upon trial."

" He says that he does not intend to surrender, that he is not afraid of the law, nor will he evade it, but he is unwilling to be taken out, stripped of his weapons and be shot down by an enraged mob."

" I will not let that be done — it shall not be done ! "

" You could not prevent it, and even if you could, he has no surety that you would. He gives his word and honor that he will not evade the law, and that he will appear at court when the trial comes up."

" My oath binds me to take him, and I intend do it, even if I have to fire the house, or go to Danville, get a cannon and *knock* it down ! "

" If you get him, you will have to pay dearly for him, and when you *do* get him, he will not be worth much. If you are his friends, he *wants* you to go away, and if his enemies, you had *better* do it ! "

" Whenever a man tells me to leave his place, I feel it my duty to do so," said William Conn.

They all followed his example, and immediately put his theory into practice. As the Doctor had determined not to be taken, he held a council with his sons and friends, to know what he had best do. As they believed their enemies had the favorable side of the law, they advised him to leave the country, for they might force him to do things which the law would not justify. His primary motive for leaving was to give the mob time to *think*, for he remembered the old adage — "A mob has many heads but no brains." He made arrangements with his sons for the preparation of his trial, and for them to send him word when it would come off, so that he might return in time. According to the advice given after deliberation, he left immediately.

THE DOCTOR'S ABSENCE.

CHAPTER VII.

The Doctor's flight — He goes to Indiana — Does not receive intelligence of his family — Sets out for home — Meets his son — The son's narrative — Hills besiege the house — Officers search for the Doctor — Gen. Dodd and the Militia — The Hills attack the boys and negroes — They shoot Thomas Evans — The Hills and sheriff's guards repulsed by the boys — Hills swear out a peace warrant against the boys, and a writ for one of the negroes — Hills attempt to set the Doctor's house on fire — News of the Lancaster fight — The Doctor returns and demands a trial — Citizens attempt to restore peace.

GENTLE READER, do not get uneasy for the Doctor's fate, for I do not intend to make a second Ulysses of him, nor a Penelope of his fair dame, although she did suffer in a different way as much persecution as the royal web-raveler.

According to the well digested advice, the Doctor crossed the Kentucky river at the mouth of Sugar creek, that night, passed through Lexington, and took breakfast beyond Georgetown the next morning. As he had many relatives in Indiana, he resolved to go there and spend the time of his exile. He visited among his friends till the first of May, and had not during all that time, received any intelligence of his family, although he had written five or six letters, and they as many more — none had been received on either side. This made him uneasy, for he knew not but what the Hills had burned his house and massacred his helpless family — hence, he determined to return and learn the state of affairs. He was within about eighteen miles of the Ohio river, on his way home, when he met his son in the road.

" Hallo son! how does it happen that I meet you here ? "

" We all became so uneasy that I was sent off in post haste to see what had become of you."

" Is the family well ? "

" We have all had excellent health."

" Well, tell me what has been going on since I left."

" We have had a pretty bitter time. The Hills have been

4

around the house all the time, and the officers have been there two or three times searching for you. The day after you left, the sheriff came down with General Dodd and a company of militia to take you. When they got to the foot of the hill, the General told the sheriff and militia to stay there, that he and William Turner would go up and get you, if they could not, no power on earth could. The General and Turner came up and asked us where you were. We told them that we did not know, that you had left for parts unknown, the night before.

" As dinner was about ready, we invited them to dine with us; they did so. Before they finished dinner, the sheriff and whole company came in, thus violating the positive orders of the General. We treated them kindly, and proposed to prepare dinner for them all, but they refused to wait, saying that their number was too great. Not long after that, one morning before daylight, the sheriff, his deputy, and some fifty men of the same *malicious* company, came back. We asked them what they wanted? They replied that they wanted to search for you, — that they had learned that you were at home. We told them that you were not there, but that they might search if they felt so disposed, and gave them a candle. They searched every room with their guns cocked, poking them about under the beds as they looked. They even looked in the hen house and smoke house, and went into the barn with lighted cigars in their mouths, as if they would slily set it on fire. Some of them went back to the house, cocked their guns at the children, and, with many wicked oaths, threatened to shoot them. The sheriff and deputy then divided the company equally among themselves. The deputy, with about thirty men, went down to Rus Hill's and took breakfast.

" After this crowd had left, and everything was quiet, Tom took the negroes and little Doc out to repair a piece of fence in the direction of Rus Hill's. The remainder of us went to work at the barn. Before they began to work, Tom went to the brow of the hill to see if they could work in safety, and to see whether the crowd were yet at Hill's. They were, and as soon as they saw him, began a brisk fire, at the distance of about three hundred yards. He told the negroes to go back home, and walked leisurely that way himself, not expecting to be followed. But the Hills and a portion of the deputy's guard came on in hot pursuit. He heard a noise and turned to see what caused it. As he turned around, they fired on him at the distance of about one hundred and five steps. An ounce ball struck him in the breast, penetrating about half an inch into the flesh and knocked him down. He arose, picked up his gun and fired back on them, then ran toward the house. Little Doc thought there would be more safety at a little distance from Tom, but that made no difference, for the balls whistled by his ears as briskly as ever. When we, at the barn, heard the shooting, and saw Tom fall, we ran instantly to the house to get our rifles, for we thought he was killed. When we got into the house, mother fastened the door and would not let us out. Just at that time Mr. Collier and his wife rode up to the gate. We told mother to go and let them in. While she was going out we got out also, and ran to meet the advancing foe. Mrs. Collier would not come in, but ran back with feminine timidity. Mr. Collier, seeing that we were about to meet the Hills, and hearing the balls whiz by and rattle on the house top, staid to witness the battle. The Hills came very near to the house and got behind a large haystack, and sent their shower of balls with renewed vigor. Sam took one of the large guns and knocked off the capping of the stack. This so much frightened them that they ran out from behind it, and as they ran, he snatched a rifle from me and fired at them, which so much augmented their terror that they did not lessen the rapidity of their flight till they got back to Hill's. For a day or two the sheriff and his *valorous* guard laid around in the neghborhood — the majority of them were beastly drunk nearly all the time. The sheriff then left them, which gave them a little more licentious liberty. They laid around the house, shot into the windows, and at any of the family whenever seen, till an angry storm drove them away. We could scarcely do any work out of doors, for they would attack and drive us from the fields whenever we attempted it. They would neither work themselves nor let us work. One day we were cutting corn stalks off the young wheat, they discovered us, and Rus Hill sent a detachment to make an attack, while he went to town and swore out a peace warrant against us, and a writ for one of the negro

boys. The officer came that night after us, and advised us to
take the negro off and sell him, for, if we did not, the Hills
would swear enough to hang him, no matter how innocent he
might be.   He then proposed to serve the warrant on us, but
we refused to surrender ourselves without he would furnish us
with a guard to accompany us to town.   He agreed to do this,
and came with a guard on the next Monday.   But we were informed that five of the Hill party had concealed themselves in
an old house on the road, to shoot at us as we passed.   When
this information was received, the neighbors, who were sum-
moned as our guard, consulted among themselves what had best
be done, and concluded to let the officers come to us and receive the bonds and security, for they knew if we went some
person would be killed.   Accordingly, the officers came and
we were placed under a heavy penalty, with good security, to
keep the peace with all mankind, and more especially with the
Hill party.   Every person then believed that the difficulty was
at an end, for the Hills were honor-bound to keep the peace in
virtue of our bonds.   And the Hills themselves expressed as
much."

"But pray, son, tell me how things are now going on at
home," earnestly inquired the Doctor.

"We get along very well, now; everything is quiet."

"Ah, I fear there is some trick in this," observed the Doctor.   "Storms are usually the burden of calms.   I very much
feared that they had burned the house down before this time.
I am sorry that you left.   We will stop at your grand-pap's
to-night; then go on in the morning."

"They did try to burn the house several times.   On one
occasion, a very dark night, I well remember, Sam took several
guns and went up into the garret to watch.   He was laying
down, watching through the little window, when he saw a coal
of fire shine in the distance.   It would disappear, as if concealed
in a vessel, or beneath the clothes of the bearer, and ever and
anon it would shine forth, to show that it had not become
extinct.   Sam understood the *movement*, and watched it
narrowly.   The bearer of the dark design came along slowly
and cautiously till he mounted the stile to cross the fence.
Here he opened the prison-gate of his fire to be sure of its

vitality. As he did this, Sam fired upon him with the large shot gun. The wretch let the fire fall, and fell himself headlong to the ground. Sam thought he was dead, and did not fire again : but after a time he crawled off like a four legged beast, doubtless not well pleased with the result of his crusade."

The Doctor and his son traveled together to Shelby county, within seventy miles of home, where one of their relatives resided. The Doctor told his son to hasten on home and prepare for his trial, while he remained for further information. The son traveled briskly, and got to Harrodsburg about dark, and there heard of the LANCASTER FIGHT. He went on immediately that night and found his brother Thomas dreadfully mutilated and not expected to live. He sent a runner to his father with the awful tidings. The Doctor received the intelligence during the following night, and set out without delay. According to an agreement of his friends, he arrived at the house of George Hackley, the constable, about ten o'clock the next night, placed himself under his care, as guard, went to Lancaster and demanded a trial. A strong guard was placed over the Doctor, not to prevent him from running away, but to afford protection against the Hills. His lawyers asked :

" Who will you be tried before ? "

" Before the two smartest judges that can be found in the county — two who know most about the law."

" Letcher and Campbell are the best judges, but we fear that Letcher is prejudiced against you."

" He has no cause for prejudice, and if he has any, I want to know it. I want to know who will act upon the principles of justice. I will take him at any rate, for this may not be the final trial."

" He went into a thorough trial before the above named judges, which lasted two or three days, and resulted in his acquittal.

The Doctor displayed considerable judgment in these maneuvers. Had he stood a trial immediately after killing Hill, he certainly would have been hanged, for the whole country was enraged against him, and the people would have had little repugnance in sacrificing him to restore peace. Peace, or war, depended upon his life. Had he been killed, his sons would scarcely have carried on the war, and the number of friends permitted to enlist in the cause was too small to prosecute it without the granite energy of their old general to stimulate them to action. But now the scales of fate turned in his favor. Every one cried out bitter anathemas against the Hills, and bade the Doctor, God speed in a cause, which excited such sympathy and intense interest in their bosoms, on account of the atrocious Lancaster fight — which will be treated of in the next chapter. Now, he could go with perfect safety into a trial, which would have formerly proven his death. This fluctuation in public sentiment affords a profound study of human nature, a study by which we may all profit. By contemplating what has past, and the *causes* that produced the events, we have a standard or guide by which we may act to create certain desirable effects, and avoid others that would be deleterious. The mind that can trace out its course in the dim future by these beacon lights, displays the true genius.

After this trial, the Hills attempted at every court to get the grand jury to indict Dr. Evans; but they passed it over in silence. The citizens then tried to restore peace, and made a proposition for the two parties to go into negotiation. The Hills pledged their word and honor that they would quit fighting if the opposite party would. The Doctor told them all they had to do was to *quit* — if they would let him alone he would extend the same favor to them — but that he could have faith in neither their word nor their honor, since they had so unscrupulously violated every principle of honor and veracity.

But for the sake of restoring peace, he agreed to visit only one half of Lancaster if they would confine themselves to the other side of town — to give half the road when they chanced to meet, and to use every means to prevent a collision between the two parties. These stipulations were equally binding upon both parties, and strictly adhered to by Dr. Evans. The future will tell how faithfully the Hills observed them.

THE LANCASTER FIGHT.

CHAPTER VIII.

HAD it been expedient to record events as they transpired, with respect to time, this scene would have come in during the Doctor's absence. But for the sake of *unity*, I thought it better to *serve* the Doctor first. The kind reader will, therefore, permit me to retrace a short period of time.

This tragical scene was acted during the Doctor's absence, in May, 1850. Sam and Tom Evans, who were respectively 18 and 16 years of age, went to town to procure some necessaries for the family, and among other things, a saddle for themselves. As they were bound under such heavy pecuniary penalties to keep the peace, they believed that the Hills were honor bound not to molest them. But notwithstanding this, they carried some of their small arms. Several of the Hill party were in the shop when the boys bargained for the saddle. In the evening, when they were ready to return home, Sam told Tom to lead the horses across the square, to the shop, while he went up stairs to get the saddle. As he approached the shop he saw a crowd of Hills standing on either side of the door, but went up without saying a word to them. Tom, leading the horses, soon followed. When he arrived at the door and saw that Sam had not come down, he thought he would hitch the horses and go up into the shop too. As he was in the act of throwing the bridles around the tree, which stood on the edge of the side-walk, the Hills rushed at him. He instantly snatched his pistol to shoot, but at that moment two or three of them fired at him, and one struck him in the forehead with a rock, which knocked him senseless. As he fell, he hollooed — " Oh Sam! Oh Sam !! " When Sam heard this and the report of the pistols, he was a few feet from the head of the stairs with the saddle on his arm — he dropped the saddle, drew a small revolver and ran down to the foot of the stairs. He saw Tom, about six feet distant to the right, with a crowd of Hills around, cutting him to pieces — some would hold while the others cut. Another group was standing on the pavement in front of the stair-way door. Just as Sam arrived at the bottom of the stairs, he saw one of the party run up to Tom and put a pistol against his head. At that instant Sam fired, struck the fellow in the right shoulder, and tumbled him, together with his pistol, into a cellar. The next moment Fred Hill run up with a bowie-knife, and was about to plunge it into Tom's breast, when Sam drove a ball into his back, and stretched him on the ground. Isaiah Hill attempted to pull Tom a little from the wall that he might have fairer *hacking*. Sam fired at his breast and struck the handle of a pistol in the right side of his coat, which so frightened him that he ran away.

The crowd before the door was placed there to shoot Sam as he came down, while the others were to do the work for Tom. At the last shot, Sam's pistol ceased to revolve, being impeded by the fragment of an exploded cap. As soon as those before the door saw this, they rushed at him, and ran up the stairs with up-raised bowie-knives, ready for a butchery. He retreated up the stairs, and by this time succeeded in getting his pistol to revolve. Rus Hill was in front, and when Sam pointed the pistol at him, he turned, tucked down his head and ran back, receiving the ball in his right shoulder. That made them scamper and clear the stair-way in double-quick time. Sam dropped the revolver on the floor, drew two single barrels, and with one in each hand, ran down to his former stand. When he got down, he saw Henry Sagracy leveling a pistol at him. At that instant Sam threw up his — Sagracy wheeled and received the ball in his right shoulder. The pistol which he held in the other hand went off and lodged its ball in the door steps. He kept pointing the empty pistol at Elijah Duggins, but found it would not fire — Duggins wheeled and ran off. He kept pointing the empty pistol at them till they all ran away. It is an extraordinary fact that they were all shot in the right shoulder. It can be accounted for only by accident, for Sam certainly did not have so much consideration and mercy as to shoot them in the right shoulder when a ball in the left side would have proven fatal. He might have aimed at the heart, but perhaps the pistol was defective, and did not throw the ball where he intended.

Sam shot two balls which he cannot account for, but John Hill confessed that one grazed his face and the other cut his hand. There were several men in the shop when the fight began, but the fear of finding a bloody grave there, forced them out of a back window and made them jump to the ground from the roof of a lofty shed-room, which seriously injured some of them. When Sam had scared all of the Hill party away, he got out at the same window, walked on the shed a little distance, raised another window and went into a room. He found there a sick young man who appeared to be very much frightened, and started to run down.

" Stop sir ! " said Sam, " you must not go down yet — help me to load my pistols. Then you must go down and tell Joshua Burdett, my lawyer, to come here ; but you must not let any one else know where I am."

The young man helped to load the pistols, and being very much agitated filled the barrels about half full of powder ; then went down through the little trap-door and did as directed. Sam had never been in the room before, nor did he know where he was ; but it happened to be a very safe place. Rus Hill was carried into the room beneath him. Sam looked at him through the cracks of the floor and could have shot him, but the groans and wailings of the wounded man touched his heart with pity. Tom was yet lying on the pavement, weltering in his inspissated gore. The Hills, after they ran away from Sam's empty pistol, went over to Yantis's drug store and got their rifles, where they had previously deposited them. They then returned and searched for Sam, and would have put an end to Tom's suffering had they not been prevented. The citizens then interposed and carried away the wounded to the different taverns.

While they were making such sad havoc with Tom, old John Hill stood near by and looked on; but as soon as he saw Sam begin to shoot them down, he cried out:

" *Lord amessy, aint there no body to stop it!* "

" Johnny, *you* had better go and stop it," observed Mr. Miller.

" Lord, I can't do nothing — I can't do nothing," replied Johnny.

And when his men began to flee before an empty pistol, he cried out:

" *Lord Jesus*, don't let him get away like his father did! "

The squad placed in front of the door to shoot Sam, fired about thirty balls at him, but not a single one touched even his clothes — they lodged in the door facings, and in the ceiling of the shop. This is an extraordinary fact, for it can scarcely be conceived how every one of such a shower of balls could miss him. Some people believe that the balls did hit him, but that he had on a shield or breast-plate, which preserved him unwounded. To this I cannot answer; but the fact of his clothes not being touched, is evidence enough that the balls would not have harmed him notwithstanding the shield. Sam thought, and said, that they were only snapping at him; but one of the party replied to this report, " Whoever said that, told a d—n lie, for I shot at him six times myself."

Burdett soon went up to where Sam was, and asked what he wanted. Sam replied:

" I want something to eat. Bring me something to eat, then prepare for my trial."

Burdett brought him some victuals — he eat composedly, then went down, delivered himself to the sheriff, and had his trial that same evening.

When the citizens interfered, the Hills swore out a writ against Sam and *Robert Collier* — swearing that they did the shooting. But when they found that Collier could prove that he was in a store on the opposite side of the square during the fight, they dismissed him and prosecuted Sam's trial. The two justices of the peace before whom he was tried, found no fault with his conduct, only that he did not do quite enough shooting, but, considering that he was a mere boy, thought it would do pretty well.

Nothing was done with the Hills; they roamed about the country unmolested, till the next court. The grand jury then indicted eleven of the party for malicious shooting and intent to kill. A portion of them came up and gave bail for their appearance at court, and were afterward tried and acquitted. The others were at perfect liberty, and cared nothing for either indictment or trial. One of the party could not give bail, but the officers did not trouble themselves about taking him. If he was thus freed from punishment by the delinquent officers of the just laws of his country, Providence had prepared a punishment for him. Soon after the fight, he was blowing rock out of a well: a blast caught before he was ready and blew him high into the air; put out his eyes, and blew his hands nearly all to pieces, rendering him perfectly helpless.

The first physician called to see Tom, said there no use in dressing his wounds, for he would be a corpse in a few minutes, and went about dressing the wounds of the more hopeful cases. Tom was most shockingly mutilated. He had four heavy cuts on the top of his head that cut through the covering of the brain, and several lighter ones on his forehead. He had received a very severe cut on the side of the head, cutting through his ear and taking off a piece of his cheek bone. One cut made a gash, immediately beneath his nose, larger than the aperture of his mouth; another severed the bone of his lower jaw. Besides several lighter cuts, he received one on his neck, which came near entirely severing the windpipe. He was indeed in a critical situation. Death seemed eager to wrap him in his cold shroud. Fate struggled against fate. The balance of human life rose and fell as if unable to decide between the weight of life and death. He was perfectly paralyzed and speechless for ten days. His spirit lingeringly hung around him, as if debating whether still to dwell in the mutilated body, or to seek an abode in brighter realms above. Four long weeks counted their weary minutes before he could be conveyed to his home. The Hills, who fell on the battle field, were confined only three or four weeks. Tom is the only one of the Evans family who received a wound during the whole war. He alone seemed to be destined to atone for all their sins. This is extraordinary, and not to be accounted for by reason; for others of the Evans family were placed in as critical circumstances, yet came forth untouched.

This battle completely changed public sentiment with respect to the two parties. Before it was in favor of the Hills, on account of Jesse Hill's death; but now, as the boys were attacked while under bail to keep the peace, the tide of public feeling reversed its course. And then the attack was so ably and bravely resisted by Sam, that he could not fail to receive the applause of a people so chivalrous as Kentuckians. He was greeted with acclamation and praise wherever met; and as testimony of the high appreciation of such rare valor, public dinners were given to him in different parts of the State. The admiration of the fair daughters of old Garrard was told in more silent but expressive strains. Every one was in a fervor of excitement to see the youthful hero — he who had vanquished a tenfold foe, and gained the field with unparalleled triumph. This battle and his valorous actions were the sweetest theme of their conversation; and to enjoy his presence was a pleasure the richest and most highly prized.

Reader, you may well imagine the feelings of a bashful and retiring boy, while these praises and commendations were floating on every breeze. It doubtless afforded him a heart-felt pleasure to see his deeds thus meet the approbation of his fellowmen; but he shrank with the timidity of a guileless maiden from such enthusiastic applause.

THE ARMISTICE.

CHAPTER IX.

THE scenes of this chapter transpired while the people believed the two parties to be under a truce, according to the stipulations agreed upon soon after the Doctor's return and trial.

After the treaty, everything seemed to be quiet for a considerable length of time. The Hills had many good reasons for desiring this armistice. As public sentiment was now so much against them, they sought every means to regain the lost good will, and for this reason made pretense that they wished to put an end to hostilities entirely and forever. But the Doctor could better fathom the depths of their dark designs. He knew that their object was to gain public favor and get a better chance to accomplish their darling wish — to take his life. They made *loud promises* to the public, yet violated the stipulations without remorse of conscience upon every occasion. Of these agreements and the small public favor gained by readily entering into them, they made an ample curtain behind which to begin again their sly and underhand work. They even frequently went in gangs, with loaded rifles as in former days, and when any of the opposite party were seen, made unmistakable show of hostilities. They caught the Doctor in town several times, and started toward him with their pistols half drawn, but when he threw his piercing eye upon them, their weak courage failed, they turned and walked off in some other direction.

The Doctor chanced to be in town one day, and Jesse Baker called on him to go a short distance into the country to see his sick wife. Several of the Hills were in town also, and had mounted their horses to return home, but they saw Baker on the corner waiting for the Doctor, and asked :

" What are you waiting for?"

" For Dr. Evans ; he is going home with me.

" Well then, we shall not go yet !" at the same time dismounting and taking a stand on the corner where they knew the Doctor would have to pass.

Baker knew their design, and ran up the street to meet the Doctor.

" You must not go this way, Doctor, for if you do the Hills will kill you. There is a crowd of them on the next corner, and they will shoot at you as you pass. Please don't go that way—go around the square and avoid them."

" Well, I am not afraid of them ; if they shoot, I can return a more destructive fire ; but they will not shoot so long as I have an eye on them."

Thus saying, he put his horse into a brisk trot, and passed them without a fire. They made several belligerent signs, and had their pistols more than half drawn ; but they could not withstand the Doctor's glance. It is a curious fact that none of the Hills could shoot at the Doctor while they could see his eye. Conscience is a powerful element in human nature—it stays in public the hand that would strike in secret.

A few days after this incident, Sam was on the creek alone, driving a herd of cattle. He saw two men not far distant down the road, apparently adjusting their pistols for a shooting exploit. As he drew nearer, he found one of them to be Rus Hill. When he came within pistol shot, they made signs of shooting, but he instantly dismounted, stood behind his horse and spoke to them :

" Take your hands out of your pockets, or go to shooting !" (They took their hands out of their pockets.) " Rus, who is that you have with you — I see he is to do all the shooting ? "

" It is Wesley Beaumont," replied Hill. But Sam soon saw his face, which proved him to be Isaiah Hill.

" Why don't you go along ?" asked Sam.

"G—d d—n you, why don't you go along?"

"I am afraid to pass, without you get out of the road."

"D—n you, did 'nt you shoot me in the Lancaster fight?" observed Rus.

"If I did, you know it, and I can do it again. I can kill you both, but I do not wish to do so."

"Well, G—d d—n you, get out of the road yourself, then."

"I will, if you will keep your hands out of your pockets till I get to that log;" pointing to a log about thirty yards from the road side.

They kept their hands out of their pockets till Sam got to the log. When they moved on and arrived opposite to Sam, Rus said:

"You are going to shoot!"

"You know that is a lie — I promised you I would not, and you know I will not break my word."

"Why don't you take your hands out of your pockets, then?"

"Because I did not promise you to do it."

They passed on without shooting, and Sam resumed the driving of his cattle. Thus it may be seen the Hills did not observe the treaty — according to which, they would have given half the road, and avoided any show of hostilities.

Subsequent to the above adventure, the Doctor met four of the party in a road. Night was just spreading her dusky mantle over the earth, as if to conceal the dark deeds of pending perfidy from mortal eye. The first whom he discovered was Henry Sagracy, on his horse a few feet from the road, raising his rifle to shoot. The Doctor knowing it to be too far to shoot with a pistol, and too close to run from a rifle, jerked his pistol from the holster, and rushed his horse directly toward him. When Sagracy saw that the Doctor could shoot first, he dropped his rifle and concealed his head and shoulders behind the horse's neck. Knowing that Hill would not shoot, the Doctor saved his load, thinking he might need it to *pepper* some of the others. He dashed on by them with his pistol half pulled off— they tucked their heads and turned their backs to the Doctor. The road was so narrow that his knee grazed them as he passed. Perhaps the reader has not discovered the ingenious reason of the Hills for turning their backs. When there was any prospect of being shot, they would invariably turn their backs toward the danger ; for had they been shot in that relative position, they could have had a pretext to swear before a court that they were retreating and had no hostile design against the opposite party — thus securing the favor of the law.   And this would have given them an apparently plausible pretext to spread reports that the Evans party had broken the treaty instead of themselves, and thus secure more of public favor.   But the Doctor had sagacity enough to interpret their untold motives.   He did not desire to kill them anyhow, for he knew that the majority of them were poor, ignorant hirelings — hired by men who apparently had little to do with the feud.   These incidents serve to show the character of the many similar occurrences that frequently happened till the Doctor accidently got his hand shot.   But notwithstanding their bold threats and cowardly attempts, the Doctor gave his sons orders strictly to observe the treaty and their bonds to keep the peace, and not to shoot if there was any possible way of avoiding it.   These orders were implicitly obeyed during the seeming armistice.   To make amends for past losses, the Doctor continued the practice of his profession, and kept the boys busy on the farm.

In the fall of 1851, old John Hill, the general of the Hill party, died.   *Rumor* says that the old man charged his son, Dr. Hill, with the crime of poisoning him, or, of giving him medicine to hasten his death, in order to come into the inheritance of his property sooner.   On this account he was dismissed from the practice in his father's family, and sent home with his wife, late one night.   When Dr. Hill went home, to Lancaster, he told Judge Letcher what had happened, and that he was accused of poisoning his father.   The Judge tried to console him by telling him that the old man was certainly deranged, or he could have no such opinion.   Hill replied that he was not deranged, nor was that the only time he had been accused of the crime.   Drs. Pierce and Hutson were then called to treat old John's case.   Under their treatment he decidedly improved.   But Dr. Hill returned soon and told the two doctors that he thought he ought to have the right of attending to his own father.   Though Dr. Pierce was by no means friendly to Dr. Hill, they relinquished the case to him willingly. After this change of physicians, old John's lamp soon ceased to burn.

After the death of John Hill, Dr. Hill assumed the command of the forces; though he kept himself in the background and denied having any participation in the feud. But actions speak louder than words. He spent nearly the whole of his time with the party and in the immediate neighborhood of Dr. Evans's residence.

About this time, January 1852, Dr. Evans had the misfortune to shoot his hand. Having returned from a visit to a patient, when he dismounted, he attempted to take his pistol from the holster, but it was frozen to the leather, and when he broke the icy cement the noise frightened the horse, and made him jump and strike the hammer of the pistol against the horn of the saddle, causing the cap to ignite and explode the powder. He happened to seize the muzzle of the pistol in his hand; the ball entered the palm and coursed down the arm, between the two bones, about seven inches. Since the ball was very large, it shockingly mutilated his hand, so much so that the attending physician said it would have to be amputated. Though it was perfectly dead, he said it should not be taken off—that he would not take the whole of Garrard county for it. It gave him intense pain, and confined him a considerable length of time.

As soon as his hand got well enough he went to see a patient, having to pass by Isaiah Hill's house. He saw a squad of Hills watching him very closely, and anticipated a difficulty on his return. He had taken Sam along with him, to open the gates, and, if needs be, to do the shooting. As they were passing through a gate, about twilight, on their way homeward, the Doctor, having gone through, heard a pistol fire, but thought that Sam had by accident fired one while shutting the gate. He soon heard another, and saw Sam's horse dash up the road. He then looked back and found Rus Hill immediately behind him. He threw the glove off his well hand, snatched his pistol from the holster, threw the bridle over the horse's head, and sprang to the ground, behind his horse. As soon as the Doctor touched the ground, Hill leveled his pistol and fired, but missed. During this time he was swearing at a wicked rate.

5

"I can whip a hundred and ninety-nine Evanses — I am *beeswax* and *rawsum* (rosin) ; by G—d—I can whip all h—ll ! " And when Sam's horse ran away with him he cried —" Come back ! Come back ! G—d d—n it, come back ! — I didn't think you were so easily scared off ! "

As soon as Sam could check his horse, he came back and asked his father :—

"Are you hurt — how came you on the ground ? "

"I am not hurt. Shoot that scoundrel, don't you see how he keeps on shooting at us ?" replied the Doctor, composedly.

Sam dashed up to Hill and fired — Hill returned the fire. Sam's horse then reared up, wheeled and ran off again. While Sam was gone, the Doctor leveled his large pistol at Hill. Hill tumbled off his horse and got behind a log, about fifty feet distant, and kept up the fire. When Sam returned, the Doctor said to him :

"Get off that horse, for you cannot manage him. Quit shooting that little revolver, take my large pistols and kill the dog ! "

Sam handed his father the bridle, took the pistols and started toward Hill. But the Doctor, seeing to what danger Sam was exposed, told him to —

"Shoot the horse down ! Don't give him that advantage of you — behind a horse and log too ! Shoot the horse down out of your way ! "

Sam would not shoot the horse, but marched directly toward Hill, under a heavy and steady fire. When he got about half way, Sam pulled trigger, but snapped — he pulled away again and took a clump of hair and skin from the top of Hill's head. The Doctor then told Sam to return and get another pistol. As they were exchanging empty for loaded pistols, Hill fired at them, then wheeled and ran off leading his horse. Sam gave chase, but Hill soon sprang upon his horse and galloped off. There was no damage done on either side, save the *minus* portion of Hill's head ; though Sam was in imminent danger when he walked out unprotected before Hill.

A few days after this incident, Dr. Evans went to Lancaster and told the Hill party, or rather, their friends, that he wanted to settle the difficulty; that he was willing to meet their best marksman anywhere and let the events of the battle-field decide the controversy; that if he came off victorious the Hill party would leave the country, if his antagonist, he and party would leave. He also left word with them that he thought Dr. Hill was the proper person to take up the challenge, since they were considered the geneials of the two parties, and that he certainly would not be such a poor, pitiful coward as to be afraid to meet a one-handed man. But the wished-for combat did not transpire, for Dr. Hill was notoriously afraid to stand before such a deadly fire as came from any of the Evans family. Had this challenge been accepted and Dr. Hill killed, it would not have terminated the tragedy, for the Hill party would not have observed the agreement; but the passion of revenge would have stirred their hearts to darker deeds.

The next occurrence happened between the Hills and Sellars. Sellars had been unfriendly with the Hills some ten or fifteen years, during which time they had many skirmishes and fights. Sellars was also an enemy to Dr. Evans, but as the war had assumed a general form, it was dangerous for him to stay at home; hence, for his own personal safety, he chose to enlist under the banner of his mildest and most honorable enemy. The Doctor was thus placed in an unpleasant position — to have an enemy in camp, one in whom he knew not how to trust.

During one evening, Sellars saw some eight or ten of the Hills pass by his house. After dark, when he supposed they were all at home, he started down the creek to attend to some business. He had not gone more than half a mile when several men, with their hands armed with rocks, stepped out from behind a large tree, and said : —

" G—d d—n you, we've got you now!"

Sellars in an instant leaped to the ground, and took shelter behind his horse. But he soon gathered up some rocks and got his horse out of the way. As he did this, one of the Hills struck him a severe blow on the arm with a rock. Sellars had the next throw — he knocked Fred Hill down, and, as he was falling, struck some of the others in the face with rocks. At that instant he heard the sound of horses' hoofs coming up the road, and supposed it to be the approach of more of the Hills. He was not deceived, for, soon, nearly the whole party arrived.

He ran to the fence, jumped over, and escaped under the cover of darkness. This is Sellars version of the affair. The Hills then reported over the country that the Doctor and his sons had waylayed them and *beat up* Fred Hill; and talked of instituting a prosecution upon that ground, but found that the innocence of the accused could be proven. Sellars sent them word that he did the work for Fred Hill. But they accused a man by the name of Murphy, then Sellars and Chrismon, and swore eternal vengeance against the latter two. They then scoured the country to find a victim to atone for the lost blood of Fred — frequently searching the houses of Sellars and Chrismon.

While the Hills were thus prowling about the country, *"seeking whom they might devour,"* Esquire Bruner, of Jessamine county, called the Doctor to see a patient. The Doctor at first refused to go—making apologies and telling him the state of affairs, and directing him where to find another physician. But the 'Squire would not hearken to these excuses, and replied : —

"The Hill party do not know my business, and we can get across the river before they can discover our design."

"Yes, that is all true, — we can cross the river very handily, but to get back again, that's the *rub*."

"Never mind that, I can furnish you with a guard of one hundred men, well armed, whose valor is as unflinching as the most tried veterans that ever trod the bloody hills of Kentucky. Your wife need not be alarmed for your safety — I will pledge myself to her for your safe return."

The Doctor finally went, and took Sam with him. They remained about three days, and set out for home in the evening— the 'Squire accompanying them. At the Doctor's urgent request to take the shot-gun along, the 'Squire laughed and said there would be no use for it. They arrived at the river, but the ferryman was absent. The ferryman had seen the Hills congregating, and knowing the whereabouts of the Doctor, suspected what was to follow, and ran away to avoid setting them over. This was very clever and generous in the ferry-man, for if he had set them across, he would have landed them in a crowd of Hills, for they were lying thick in ambush on the opposite shore; and there would have remained little hope for the Doctor with his short arms in opposition to such an unequal foe with their long guns. They stood on the river bank some time and called the ferryman, but to no avail. Sam went down to the ferryman's house to see if he could be found there, but, as was afterward learned, he had left, through fear of the Hills, for they had threatened to kill him if he did not set the Doctor across.

The Doctor laid down on the bank to rest, and soon saw that it would not be expedient for them to cross. He saw several groups lying in concealment, and watched them change their locality as cautiously as a flock of quails would before a fowler. 'Squire Bruner saw another group, but, not suspecting anything, thought it was some of the ferryman's friends coming to set them across. Only a few minutes had elapsed when the Doctor heard a rifle fire, and a ball whiz by his head. This opened the 'Squire's eyes to the reality of the case, and he wanted to get away without delay. In order to deceive the Hills, they went down the river, as if aiming to cross at the lower ferry, till they came to a secluded path that led back to the 'Squire's. They returned to Bruner's as quickly as possible, for they feared the Hills would cross the river and give chase. As the Hills were running down to the other ferry, several people saw them and asked where they were going. They replied : —

"We have started an *old buck* up the river, and are running down to head him at the next ferry."

When they got there, they hid themselves in the bushes, and awaited the expected arrival of the *buck*. It is believed that they stationed half of their forces at one ferry and half at the other, and remained there the entire time of the Doctor's absence. Bruner, not being used to the wiles of the Hills, found himself dreadfully puzzled how to secure the Doctor's return home.

" I have you here now, and I have pledged myself to your wife for your safe return. You know more about the maneuvers of the Hill party than I do, so choose your way home and I am at your service. I will furnish you with as many men and rifles as I promised, and more if needed."

" I know you will do whatever you promise Squire ; but

since you have left it to me, I wish to start in the morning about two o'clock. I want only two men, of the *right sort*, with the right sort of rifles. We will go lower down and cross on the bridge, for they cannot hide there, and if they meet us on the bridge, we can whip them."

With the guards, the Doctor set out for home, and arrived without further molestation.

THE SCOTT'S FORK TRAGEDY.

CHAPTER X.

WHEN the Hills heard that the Doctor had succeeded in
getting home, they left the river, and went in search of Sellars
and Chrismon. They went to Sellars's house — but he saw them
coming, and ran away. Then they proceeded to Chrismon's —
who hid himself in the garret, and thus eluded a battle. They
kept up this hunt till the battle known as the Scott's Fork
tragedy.

On the evening before this battle, Sellars and Chrismon went
over to the Doctor's and told him —

"We have been running from the Hills so much, that we cannot run any longer — we are perfectly broken down, and have
determined to run no more."

"You had better keep out of their way — you had better
continue yet to run ; for if they catch you, there will be little
hope for your escape ! " replied the Doctor.

"It makes us feel so mean, cowardly, to be always run and
dogged in this manner. We would rather die a brave death,
than to be thus chased like infamous cowards — and, in fact,
we are unable to run any longer. We have only one rifle
apiece ; and these, you know, could make little resistance
against such a number as are thirsting after our blood. Now,
as you have an abundance of arms — just look around, the
walls are studded with them — we want to borrow another gun
apiece."

"I cannot part with any of my guns; I have not enough for my own defense."

"You *must* lend to us, for you can borrow as many as you need, and more too ; but no one will lend to us, and we have not the money to buy them."

"I will have need for all the guns at my command. Now, as you have been running so much, and as you are too much worn out to fight, you had better stay here with me. We will protect you, for the Hills will not dare come here."

"But we must be at home — we have to prize our tobacco to-morrow. We have sent word to the Hills, that if they will let us prize our tobacco and sell it, we will leave the country immediately — we told them we wanted only time to wind up our business."

"You had better leave as soon as possible ; for I fear they will not grant you this short respite."

"Then if they attack us, we would have a better chance to protect our lives with two other guns. They are likely to attack us in the tobacco house, while we are at work there ; and if we had more guns we could give them a hotter battle — we can whip them at any rate — intend to try it if they make the attack."

"You had better not attempt it. It would be bloody work. Such a company, even if they were the basest cowards, can with ease whip two men so scantily armed. And there is Chrismon, he cannot kill a man — he cannot fight that kind of a fight. The materials of which he is composed are too tender for such hardihood — his nerves could not withstand such a contest. He would rather kill himself — his nature is too good and benevolent for the iron disposition of the world. If he had all the Hills tied out there to an apple tree, he could not kill one by shooting all day. But you, Sellars, have the heart of a lion, and can give the enemy their dues. But against such odds, I would advise you to avoid a contest."

"You are mistaken, Doctor, about Chrismon ; he has more nerve than you imagine."

"That matters not; if I err, it is on the safe side. One man cannot whip such a gang, but two can, if they fight right. Keep on running till my hand gets well, then you (Sellars), and I will meet them anywhere. But if the fight *must* come up, get Sam to help you — you and he can whip them in any situation."

· " *But we must have the guns!* " said Sellars, picking up two, one a very large shot-gun.

" I cannot spare them."

" We can get guns nowhere else — you can borrow fifty, and by G–d we intend to have these — you had better not offer resistance. This is the very big shot-gun that I wanted — it is the only gun that can burst that iron shield off of Rus Hill, and by G–d I intend to have it. Now let Rus try to run me any more, if he wants his iron skin pierced ! "

Thus saying, Sellars walked off with the guns. The Doctor did not want to resist him, for he feared to stir up old animosities.

Late next evening, after the above conversation, Jack May rode up to the Doctor's in great haste and excitement, and told him that Sellars and the Hills were fighting — that the Hills, about twenty strong, had besieged Sellars and Chrismon in the tobacco house, and were shooting at them as fast as they could load.

Upon the reception of this intelligence, the Doctor told his sons to get their rifles and run over to assist Sellars. But when they arrived, the battle had terminated, the Hills were all gone, and some of the neighbors were hauling off Sellars and Chrismon on a slide. The boys returned home and reported the misfortunes of the day.

We derive a description of the battle from the testimony of both parties, as given in court.

On the morning of the 13th of March, 1852, the Hill party desired to move John Brown down to Isaiah Hill's place. A portion of the party, under the command of Dr. Hill, armed themselves well with guns, pistols, bowie-knives, etc., and went along with the wagon. Their road led by the tobacco house in which Sellars and Chrismon were prizing tobacco. In the morning, when they passed, Sellars and Chrismon ran away and hid themselves in John Warren's house, which was near by. The party went on together to Teetersville, where a portion of them remained to indulge in the delights of bacchus, till the others returned with Brown and his furniture. Before leaving the village, they replenished their copious jugs with the maddening fluid, and often, during the journey, held *communion* with the *spirits*. They told Thomas Warren to tell John Warren not to let Sellars and Chrismon conceal themselves in his house any more, for on returning they were determined to take them, even if they had to pull the house down.

James Alverson, Sellar's uncle, and Sam Sellars, his brother, on hearing that Sellars and Chrismon were preparing to stand their ground, tried to persuade them not to have an engagement with the Hills, but to run away as they had done previously. But before their persuasion had the desired effect, a gun was heard a few hundred yards up the creek, which was known to be a gun of the approaching party. They still continued their entreaties, but in reply were told it was too late then to retreat. While the Hills were gone, Sellars and Chrismon put the house in a more defensible condition, closing the apertures between the logs with fence-rails, etc., and making port-holes through which to shoot. As the party approached, Alverson sat down in the door, Chrismon on a bulk of tobacco in the back part of the house, Sam Sellars beside a hogshead of tobacco, and John Sellars stood, with rifle in hand, watching at one of the portholes. When the Hills got within shooting distance of the house, Henry Sacracy and Rus Hill fired and wounded Chrismon in the bowels. John Sellars then fired and killed Rus Hill. When they saw that their men could be thus easily plucked from their midst, they became frightened and turned to flee. But Dr. Hill ordered them to storm the house, else they would all be killed. They then ran up to the house. Dr. Hill kept Brown's wife and the wagon between himself and danger till he got past the house, then got down and hid behind a log. When the party surrounded the house and were shooting through the cracks, Alverson arose from the door-sill and received a ball in his wrist. This one was enough of *lead pills* for him, and induced his legs to do him good service in carrying him as fast as possible to Warren's house. Sam Sellars imitated the example of his uncle, and like him, concealed himself in the garret; but as he ran, a ball gave him a slight cut across the abdomen, which doubtless increased his velocity. The fight still raged with fierceness. When the balls began to come in

too thick and fast to be comfortable, John Sellars jumped out
at the door and killed Jim Hill. Then Isaiah Hill and Sellars
had a chase around a hogshead of tobacco that was under prize.
While this race was going on, Dr. Hill called Sam Hill to get
his pistols and help Isaiah, his father. Sam got the Doctor's
pistols, ran up and shot at Sellars, but at that instant Isaiah
fell before a fatal ball. Sellars then turned and bursted two
caps at Sam — but while he was doing this, Sam shot him twice.
At the second fire, Sellars seized his gun and run. As he
was running off, John Brown shot him in the back, which
caused him to throw his gun into the weeds, stagger back a few
paces, and fell. When he fell, Bill Hill ran up, put a revolver
against his head and shot six balls through his brain. John
Brown then ran up with a bowie-knife and stabbed him two or
three times in the breast. He would twist the knife around,
then hold it up to the sun, and was almost frantic with ecstasy
to see the large drops of blood trickle from its point. Some of
the *young stock* satiated their vile revenge upon the dead body
by brutally mangling it with knives. Fred Hill and two or
three others ran into the house to bring Chrismon to a savage
death. As they came, he shot at Fred and grazed his head,
which knocked him down. The others fired on him several
times, setting his clothes on fire, and literally cutting him to pieces
with their knives. He begged for mercy, but they told him to
beg his God — that they had no mercy for him. After they
had thus dreadfully mutilated him, they took his rifle, pistol and
bowie-knife, and the large shot-gun which belonged to Dr.
Evans.

After this bloody work was finished, Dr. Hill, still lying
behind the log, hallooed and told them that the Evanses were
coming, and if they did not get away very quickly they would
all be killed. They were about to fly and leave their dead on
the field, but Jim Hill, a lad, swore that he would not leave the
ground without the body of his father — that he would die
before he would leave it. They ordered Sam Preston, a
neighbor, to drag the body to the fence, being afraid to do it
themselves. He told them that it was extremely wrong for
them to make him do that which they themselves were afraid to
do. But Jim, fearing the speedy arrival of the Evanses, drew

his pistol and told them if some one did not help to get his father away, he would fire upon the crowd. They then hastily dragged the bodies to the wagon, threw them in like so many hogs and made a quick retreat. When they arrived at their *camp*, they threw the bodies down on the entry floor and let them remain there all night without any attention. The wounded one got well in a few weeks and said that he did not mind taking *leaden pills* — that he could take them with ease, even *without water*. The next day, while yet the dead bodies were kicked about on the floor, they swore that they would kill Jack May for telling the Evanses of the attack, and that they would also kill Mr. Hall, John Warren and Henry Brookshire. They laid around these men's houses, with their rifles. This so much frightened them, and pictured such a bloody future, that nearly, if not quite all of them left the country immediately.

After this battle, some person asked Dr. Hill if the fighting would not terminate at this : "No," replied he, "by G—d, it is just begun. I intend to survey around these hills and whip every one of the d—n rascals or drive them from the country." The Evans party then went about the country two or three days, with their rifles, desiring a combat, till Dr. Evans persuaded them to desist and stay at home. He told them that court would be holden in May, and then all the Hills would be indicted for willful murder and sent to jail. But the boys knew better about the state of affairs, and the fear that the officers had for the Hills. The Hill party made no cessation of hostilities, but swore that they would storm the house, go in and get the Doctor, cut out his heart, and sport it in triumph through the country on a pole.

THE EVENTS OF BEDSTER'S DEATH

CHAPTER XI.

NOT long after the Scott's Fork tragedy, Dr. Hill received a supply of new troops, from Washington county, known as the Washington troops, or Washington recruits. They were a set of low-bred fellows, loafers, and rioters by profession at home, and hired to fight at fifteen dollars per month, with a standing reward of five dollars extra for a scalp of the Evans party.

One evening Dr. Hill mustered his forces, and sent Dr. Evans word that he wanted to quit fighting — that he had never had any hand in the fight, and that he did not wish to have any thing whatever to do with it. In reply, Dr. Evans sent him word that he was a liar — that he was the leader of the band, and had pretended for the last three years to have a right to shoot at him — that he was now at liberty to use his pretended right, for there was not room enough on the top of the ground for both of them in Garrard county. They continued their old practice of waylaying the roads, and laying around Dr. Evans's house, shooting at any of the family, or party, whenever seen.

In May, the grand jury indicted a good many of them for killing Sellars and Chrismon, but the county court granted them bail. After giving bail, they resumed the war with renewed vigor. They watched the fields, and when any of the Evans boys attempted to work, they attacked and drove them home. On this account, they were compelled to keep out a strong guard all the time. Thus, so many sentries were required that few of the party remained to till the crop. Soon, the Hill party increased to such a number that none of the Evanses could work — they could not do more than protect themselves.— Hence, they stayed at home, pretty well confined to the house, and did not venture out in several days.

One afternoon at dinner, during this inactivity, Sam seemed almost delirious — the augmenting troubles bore so heavily upon his mind. He observed to the other boys, as they silently masticated their cheerless repast:—

" Boys, let us wipe up our guns and take a *squirrel* hunt this evening, for we must drive them devils off somehow! We are not able to whip the whole party ourselves, at least, so long as they can hire half of Washington county to help them, so we must see who will help us ! "

They put their guns in shooting order, and went over to Capt. Murphy's. They stayed there all night, and returned next morning with three or four other men — Jack May being one of the number. On Sunday morning they all left except May, and he told the Doctor:—

" I am afraid to stay at home — they have been laying around my house for some time, and shooting at me every chance. You know I have but an indifferent log cabin — they can go into it any time, take me out and serve me like they did Sellars and Chrismon."

" You are welcome to stay here, if you are afraid to stay at home," replied the Doctor.

Reader, you have, doubtless, watched the conduct of the two parties, with scrutiny, up to this period. The Hills, you have seen, were perfectly abandoned to all the vices to which the human race is heir — possessed of hearts dead to all the holy principles of humanity and rectitude, and minds regardless of the mandates of honor, and uninfluenced by those higher qualifications which are characteristic of a lofty soul. They took every advantage, no matter how low and mean, waylaid the roads, besieged the house at night, and spread reports that were as false and base as the hearts that gave them birth. On the other hand, you cannot have failed to admire the straightforward and honorable course of the Evans party. By this, it is not intended to be said, that the Evans party never did anything wrong during the war; for it is a moral impossibility for any man, or set of men, to go through such protracted excitement and danger, without doing that which staid and sober men might pronounce blameable. But so far as my information extends, they never condescended to practice the low tricks of which the enemy were so fond. They never laid in ambush about either house or road; nor did they begin a fight, or intentionally place themselves in such a situation as would bring on a rencounter. Indeed, it was almost impossible for them to be guilty of such mean conduct, for their number was so very small that they were compelled to act entirely on the defensive, and had not the men to thus vigorously prosecute the war. So far as was practicable and safe, they attended to their different occupations, and never collected in bands, unless forced to do so by an attack of the enemy. But henceforth, you will perceive them act in the offensive as well as the defensive. This course of conduct was necessary for their safety, and the only means of bringing the feud to a close. Sam's remark, on an evening previous, that they would have to run the Hills off, led their minds to these conclusions, and marks a grand division in the events of our little history. Hence, from this time forth, they tried to surprise the enemy and kill them at every opportunity, for they knew this was the only way to rid the country of the pest. They did not, however, resort to any contemptible stratagems to deceive the enemy, but often went in companies to give more decisive battles.

A few days after the Evanses had resolved upon their future mode of carrying on the war, the Doctor wanted some of the necessaries of life for his family, and remarked to the boys, as they sat gloomily around :—

" Boys, since the Hills have possession of Lancaster, which

prevents us from going there, will you go over to 'Squire Bruner's and get me some little things ? "

" Father we are afraid to go.   We have but little ammunition and cannot begin to resist such a host as will come upon us."

" It is true that you have not an abundance of ammunition, but I will risk the chances of your whipping the whole party when commanded by such a piece of cowardice as Dr. Hill. But you can go through the woods to Richardson's ferry and cross the river before they can learn that you are out.   You must not let them know that I am here alone, for they might storm the house and kill me and the little children, and I know they would not have humanity enough to spare your mother.

" We will go, but dread it.   It is certain if we do not go and get something to subsist upon, we will starve.   There are only two alternatives—we had better run a risk in getting food than meet the sure fate of starvation."

" Very well, but if the Hills learn that you have gone, they will waylay the road on your return.   For this reason you had better return by way of Teeter's ferry, and thus avoid them."

The boys went and procured the necessaries as directed by their father.   On their return, about dusk, they* met two of the Hill party, Nelson Sutherland, (better known by the illegitimate name of Bedster,) and Jim Hill, not far from the mouth of Sugar creek, at the junction of Scott's Fork, near 'Squire Level's house.   The boys saw them first, about sixty yards distant, and as Bedster was a few paces before Hill, they raised their guns and fired upon him.   Bedster raised his gun and was in the act of shooting when the balls struck him, causing him to wheel, run about a hundred yards and fall.   Jim Hill leaped into a deep ravine beside the road and fired at them with a double-barrel shot-gun, then wheeled and ran back toward the creek.   They gave him a hot chase for about three hundred yards, and shot him in the hip, which brought him to the ground.   They shot him again through the thigh as he fell, and would have killed him, but his supplications for mercy stayed the blood-thirsty dagger.   They were more than anxious to kill

* The Doctor is not responsible for these facts, for they were not proven in court, but I can assure the reader that the *boys* did kill Bedster.   I gained the information from a reliable source.

him, but his prayers for mercy touched their hearts with compassion.

Now look at the contrast between the two parties! When Chrismon was lying in a helpless condition with a mortal wound in his bowels, he besought them to have mercy, but they told him that they had no mercy, that he must pray to his God for mercy. When the Evanses had one of the enemy in their power, and could have plunged a knife to his heart, his implorings moved them to pity, even after they had sworn unrelenting vengeance.

When Bedster fell, he had a rifle, a Colt's large repeater, two single-barrel pistols, and a very large bowie-knife. The pistols and knife were worn in a belt, in regular land-pirate fashion. Upon examination, Dr. Hill said that four rifle balls passed through his heart, several went into his neck, and others struck the gun stock.

Several of the Hill party said they were near by and saw the fight, and recognized every one of the Evans party at the distance of three or four hundred yards. Others said they ran three-quarters of a mile to him, after he fell, and that he was yet alive and talked to them, telling that the Evans party killed him, and of whom the party was composed. Now we can scarcely believe this. To believe that he ran even a hundred yards after four large rifle balls had mutilated his heart, is as much as my credulity can support. But it would have been a miracle had he lived longer than a man could run three-quarters of a mile. What think you, reader? The Hills immediately swore out a warrant and had the boys tried before two justices of the peace, Kurty and Terrel. The trial resulted in an acquittal, doubtless, for the want of reliable testimony.

The Hills kept pretty closely forted up all summer. They staid principally at Dr. Hill's in Lancaster, but made frequent excursions through the country in search of the enemy. The houses of Fred and Bill Hill were also converted into forts, rendering convenient service as *military* stations, forts, arsenals, magazines etc., when they chanced to go out on an expedition. Since they thus had possession of Lancaster, Dr. Evans could not go there to prosecute his suits against them, but they could prosecute him, or party, and not even permit him to be at the trial.

6

While out on these scouring expeditions they were usually drunk, at least the majority of them were, and would shoot at people who happened to resemble any of the Evans party. They shot at a certain doctor several times, supposing him to be Dr. Evans — and a young man, resembling one of the boys, was in imminent danger, for pistols were frequently presented at him, and bowie-knifes often glittered in the light, ready to make sad havoc with an innocent victim. In fact, no one was certain of personal safety in such a condition of affairs. They knew not how soon a ball from some drunken marksman, might sap their heart's blood, nor could their feelings be free from fear that a revengeful assassin might spring from his covert and make a life pay the forfeit of some careless expression, or a just desire to put an end to the feud by bringing both parties rigidly to justice.

In view of these facts, the people held a public meeting in August, at Lancaster, to devise means to put an end to a war so dangerous to themselves, and so detrimental to the character and prosperity of their county. It had such a powerful influence upon the community that several men removed from the county to get rid of the excitement and danger. And its influence was equally as powerful abroad, for if a Garrard man happened to be crowded in a street or any public place, if he wanted elbow-room, all he had to do was to tell those near him that he was from Garrard county. The knowledge of this simple fact would procure him all the room that he could desire, for they feared to be near Garrard people, having heard so much of their wide-spread fame for a warlike and fierce disposition. The meeting passed a resolution that they would henceforth, strictly execute the law on both parties. There were several gaseous speeches on the occasion, but their weight if they had any, was not felt, for *buncombe* speeches are usually as light as hydrogen.

Dr. Evans then wrote a letter to Dr. Hill, proposing to settle the difficulty — stating that if they, the Hills, would give bond and security to keep the peace, the war should cease. Dr. Hill wrote back in reply that he would not leave the settlement of the feud to Dr. Evans's arbitrary dictation, but that he would leave it to some of the good citizens to say what should

done. Accordingly, they respectively chose two men to act
arbitrators. This committee wrote several propositions, or
icles of agreement, before they could get one to meet Dr.
l's approbation. They were honest and honorable men, and
y anxious to settle the difficulty, hence, they kept changing
 propositions till they finally succeeded in getting one that
, Hill would sign. They then carried the proposition down
Dr. Evans, to get his signature. When he read it he re-
rked:—

" I might as well sign away my life at once. It only binds
upon our word and honor. Now, you know that these Hills
ve no veracity, and that they are as devoid of honor as the
vil is of righteousness — and you know, furthermore, that we
l preserve inviolate any stipulation entered into by me.
eir pledge is worthless, for they have no honor to pledge;
l if they have, I would not trust them. I want stronger
ds than their mere promise. The article binds us to lay
wn all arms, and use none under any pretext whatever.
m this, their design is very evident — it is a scheme to take
 life, while I am totally unarmed. They would not observe
but would shoot me down at first sight. But if you say I
st sign it, I will do so."

After this exposition of the nature and consequences of such
stipulation, they did not desire his signature. Dr. Evans
nt to town the next day and tried to get a reconsideration.
e arbitrators chosen by the Hill party at first agreed to a
onsideration, but afterward refused, being advised by Dr.
ll. Dr. Evans then consulted his friends to know whether
 should sign the articles of agreement as they stood. They
vised him not to do it. This circumstance gave the Hills a
orable opportunity of spreading false reports — making loud
etensions that *they* were anxious to settle the feud. These
orts had some weight with the people, and in some degree
ned the tide of public sentiment, for they, apparently, were
pported by facts.

The regular time for court soon came on, and the grand jury
licted the boys for killing Bedster.

On the same day of the indictment, I presume, the Doctor
d his sons went to a public sale. They met there Joe

Murphy, one of the Hill party, who pretended that he wished to become friendly. But the Doctor would hold no conference with him, believing that he wanted only to get a good opportunity to shoot. He told Murphy's friends if they would go his security that he had no malicious design in thus trying to make friends, that he would come to terms of conciliation. But his friends would not go this security. The Doctor then told them that he did not want Murphy to speak to him, nor come near enough to shoot. Murphy swore to his friends that he had no weapons of any kind whatever. But this was soon proven false, for he was seen behind a tree trying to shoot one of the Doctor's sons. His friends told him that he had better leave the place and go home. He swore by G—d if he had to run away from a place on account of Dr. Evans, he would go home, arm himself, and kill every one of the Evans party that he could find. Accordingly he went home, got his rifle, and concealed himself in a cornfield near the road, which it was supposed the Doctor would pass on returning home. But fortunately he did not get to his ambush till the Doctor had passed.

While the Doctor was yet at the sale, the sheriff approached him, and said:

"I am sorry that your boys have come here to-day, I have an indictment against them, and it is my duty to take them."

"There they are," replied the Doctor, "you can take them. We have been dodging from the Hills, but we do not intend to dodge the law, or its officers."

"It will not make much difference with the boys anyhow, for your lawyers are making arrangements to have their trial on next Wednesday."

"They will go with you now, or at any future day you may propose — they are not afraid of the law. But you must let them carry their arms to defend themselves against the Hills."

"I would like to have them on next Wednesday at the trial."

"Very well, we will meet you in Lancaster on that day, if you will say nothing to the boys about it. To mention it to them would do no good, but make them a little uneasy perhaps, and unruly."

The Doctor went with the boys to Lancaster, according to

promise, but the Hills put the trial off till Saturday, pretending not to be prepared to prosecute it. When he found that the trial had been deferred till Saturday, the Doctor asked the sheriff to let the boys go back home with him. The sheriff replied :

" I cannot possibly let them go. The Hills are already slandering me for letting them have too much liberty."

" Do you not believe that the boys will return on Saturday ?"

" I have not a shadow of a doubt on that point. But rather than be slandered, as I know I will be, if I let them go, I would rather keep them here in the hotel and pay their board myself."

" You can let them go home with a guard — I will board guard and all for nothing. The Hills know that I will have to attend the trial on Saturday, and they will attempt to kill me if I venture to come alone. I am afraid to go home by myself, for it is impossible for me to get there without being shot at. You have no reason for detaining them here, for you know they will come at the time appointed, as certain as the decrees of heaven."

" You know it is not pleasant for an officer to be slandered on account of not performing his duty. They must *not* go ! "

The Hills expected Dr. Evans to return that evening, and intended to waylay the road, and left Bill Hill, the Doctor's brother, in town to watch him, and give the signal of his departure, that they might be ready for his approach. The Doctor finally set out for home, but rode so briskly that Hill did not have time to give the warning till he had passed. Thus, had Bill Hill been a little more expedite, the Hill party would have been ready, and Dr. Evans death would have been almost inevitable. But Providence disposed otherwise.

I am of opinion that the sheriff had no good reason to support his conduct toward the boys. If the boys were subject to his custody, it seems evident that he should have lodged them in jail, instead of in a public tavern. If he had the power to let them remain at a tavern, he had the power to let them go home under a guard. But correct actions could scarcely be expected under such prevailing excitement.

Now, as the Doctor had succeeded in getting home, it was a matter of much doubt whether he could return to Lancaster on the appointed Saturday, for the Hills had all their plans mature, and all their men well trained in their respective parts of the expected tragedy. But at the appointed time several neighbors came in to accompany him, and do the office of guard. His company was also augmented by several witnesses in the pending suit, and those of his party not in the custody of the sheriff. The company was about to set out without their rifles, but the Doctor begged them not to be guilty of such folly.

"You had better take along your long guns, for we will be attacked, and some of us killed before we get to Lancaster."

"Oh, it will look too bad for a company of armed men to ride into town in this manner! It will prejudice the people against you, and have an unfavorable influence in the boys' trial."

"If you don't take them, I will not go, for we will have bloody work before we get there — some of us will be killed!"

"Why don't *you* take long arms then?"

"Because I can use short arms better. I cannot yet well use my wounded hand. If you don't take them, some of us will be killed as sure as the sun shines."

"If any body gets killed, it will be you."

"I know they will shoot at me, but you know they are marksmen not remarkable for precision, and might do a bad piece of work for some of those near me."

The Doctor could not prevail on them to carry any long guns, and they started off with only small arms. When they had gone a few hundred yards, he called them together to hold a council about the mode of defence, should they be attacked. As they had ever considered him their general, they left the matter with him. He told them: —

"It is far better to fight bravely than to run cowardly. In the one case you have a chance to kill an enemy, in the other, only a chance to get killed yourself. If they attack us, the the first one that sees where the shots come from, must fire in that direction, then the whole party will gallop up near enough to shoot with our small arms. When we get within pistol shot, we must jump down behind our horses and fight with the bravery of the world-renowned Spartans. If we do this they will get the worst of the battle."

They rode along without any molestation till they got nearly to Lancaster, within sight of Dr. Hill's house. As they approached, they noticed a considerable stir and excitement about the premises. There were a great many people in the road, going to hear the trial. 'Squire Kurtz, Hackley, and Dr. Tillett were riding along abreast — Dr. Evans rode up on the right hand side, (the house being on the left,) and observed : —

" Good morning, gentlemen ! I believe I will take shelter behind you till we get past the *fort*. They certainly will not kill three clever men to get one bad one ! "

" Oh, I reckon there's no danger ! " — replied one of them.

" Yes there is danger, and *considerable* danger too. If we give them only half a chance you will hear the battle's roar."

When they had passed the house some distance, far enough to be out of danger of balls coming from thence, the Doctor fell back into his own company, with James Brim on his right side and Jesse May on the left. As soon as he resumed his position, he heard a gun fire. The report was very singular, apparently deadened by being in a hole in the ground. The Doctor thought that it could scarcely be shot at them, but checked his horse and turned to see if he could discover the locality of the shooter. At that instant another gun fired, which convinced the Doctor that they were shooting at him and his company. He then commanded his company to charge on the house — at the same time wheeling his horse in that direction. But to his consternation, when he looked to see if his company obeyed the command, he saw them all running away, save Bill Murphy, who was looking up into a tree, believing them to be up there concealed in the leaves. At that instant another gun fired, and he observed to Murphy : —

" Let's go away from here, we can't see where the shots come from ! "

The Doctor wheeled his horse and galloped up the road. At that instant two more balls were fired at him. James Brim and Jesse May were riding on some distance ahead. When the Doctor overtook them, May observed : —

" Doctor, they have hit me — they have killed me ! "

" I hope not, Jesse. Hold on and ride fast ! "

" Indeed ! indeed they have, Doctor — they have *killed* me !"

They were all in a brisk lope, but May checked his horse and reined him to one side of the road, and was apparently falling. The Doctor rode up to his side and caught him as he was falling, but at that moment another gun was fired at him. As Hackerly was near by the Doctor asked him to take care of May, if he pleased, — that they would not shoot him. When Hackerly turned to May another gun fired.

The Doctor's sons at the tavern, heard the shooting and ran down to meet them. The Doctor told them to go back, that they had no arms, but to go back and arm themselves with rifles, then hunt for the concealed marksmen. They went back. May was carried into town, but did not speak another word after the Doctor left him, and died in half an hour. James Brim had a ball pass through the breast of his coat, but it did not cut his flesh.

There were two of the Hill party, Ples Huffman, and one of the young Hills, stationed in an old well, near the road, to shoot at the Doctor as he passed. This accounts for the dead sound of the gun's report. Dr. Hill and Joe Murphy were lying behind the fence, and covered over with weeds that had been cut down a day or two before. Others of the party were scattered along the fence towards town.

When the court heard of this affair, it immediately ordered out a writ for the capture of Dr. Hill and Joe Murphy, or rather, sent the sheriff to take them. The sheriff went, but soon returned and said that they would not surrender, and that their number was so great he could do nothing with them. The Doctor told the sheriff to tell the judge to let his boys loose and they would soon trot the defaulters up to justice. The judge sent word to the Hills, by the sheriff, that if they did not surrender, he would turn the Evanses loose on them. This piece of intelligence breathed a spirit of submission into their hearts. This fatal affair caused intense excitement and wild confusion, so much so that the court adjourned, and had no trial on that day. People were running to and fro in breathless excitement, and scarcely knew what they did, heard, or saw.

The Hills, in this action, shot at May and Gordon in particular, for they were the principal witnesses in the pending suit. But they did not succeed in their design upon Gordon.

After this event the sheriff admitted that the Doctor knew more about the wiles and tricks of the Hill party than he did, and consented to let the boys return home to attend the funeral of May. He furnished them with rifles, accompanied them home, left them there in perfect freedom, and went about his business.

On the following Monday, the sheriff returned and the whole party went to town with as many arms as they could carry. The trial came up on that day. Information was received the next morning before court convened that the Judge had deter mined to throw the boys in jail till the next court. When this was made known, the Doctor asked them if they would go to jail.

"Yes," replied they, "if the *judge* says so." They were accordingly put in jail.

The reader cannot fail to notice the injustice practiced here. In a similar case, when the Hills killed Sellars and Chrismon, they were allowed bail and permitted to go at large. But now, as the Evanses were in custody, there was no law to give *them* bail. The assigned reason for this partiality was, that the officers, prior to that time, had not done their duty, but that thenceforward they intended to do their duty rigidly. I am of opinion that it is a poor set of officers that will swerve from their duty under any circumstances. But they were not so much to blame in this particular case, for the whole country was in such a fever of excitement that scarcely any one knew right from wrong.

Thus the Doctor was left alone to carry their horses and arms back home. He asked some of his neighbors to help him, but they had justly grounded fears and declined granting such a dangerous favor. Finally, he succeeded in getting two, Joe Ray and Robert Collier, to assist him. His friends tried to persuade him not to return home that night, for they feared he would be killed on the road. He replied that he would return to his family or die in the attempt. When the shades of night became sufficiently dense to afford the Doctor a protecting ob- scurity, he mounted his horse, and, with a few scared friends, went up the Richmond pike a short distance, to deceive the

Hills, should they be watching, then turned across the country and arrived safely at home.

Dr. Hill and Murphy were now in custody; but, as the sheriff had allowed the Evans boys so much liberty, they claimed the same as a right. Their trial came off the next day before two justices of the peace, and as they both claimed the honor of killing May, both were sentenced to jail. Now, they were about to get into a terrible condition — about to be put into the same room with their deadly enemies, or down into the lightless dungeon. But they got out a writ of habeas corpus. and, by some ingenuity, put off their trial from time to time — and, in the mean while, tried to find some law to put themselves into another jail, but could not succeed. Dr. Hill said he was afraid to go in with the boys, and would pay any expense incurred in putting himself into any other jail. In virtue of the writ of habeas corpus, and the former leniency of the sheriff, aided by the desire of the community not to put the two parties together, they were still permitted to stay at home with their arms, till one morning they were numbered among the *missing*. As soon as the Governor was informed of this fact, he offered a reward of $200 for the apprehension of each of the runaways.

Though the sheriff knew not their whereabouts, they did not leave their old range, but laid around Dr. Evans's during the night, and kept *dark* at their *forts* in the day time. Thus they proved as much annoyance to the Doctor as ever. They laid around and shot at the house till they became weary of that sport, then they tried their skill upon the cattle and other stock in the fields. This state of affairs continued several weeks, and the Doctor thought they would kill him *anyhow*, notwithstanding his great precaution. But all human action is destined to have an end. One morning, after they had made their balls rattle upon the house with more than usual vigor, one of the Doctor's little boys, about ten years of age, and the only one left at home, was out in the yard cutting wood. He was seen to become suddenly restless, as if driven almost to desperation, while from his eyes flashed a reckless passion. It was known that the oppressive wrongs endured by his family, had wrought his soul to the highest degree of intensity, and that ne was determining upon a plan to avenge himself. His mother was watching him. He disdainfully threw down the ax and walked off around the house, whistling a careless air, as if to conceal the emotions that agitated his mind. He was observed to slip slily into the house and get the large Mississippi rifle, then slip out again cautiously toward Bill Hill's, as if he wished no one to see him. Soon a report of the rifle was heard. He had gone down to Bill Hill's and concealed himself in ambush to try his skill in the arts of war. He had not been in this covert long, before a man, supposed to be Bill, came out of the house and went into a workshop near by. As he returned to the house and stepped to the door, Doc, for that was the little boy's name, let old Mississippi loose on him and tumbled him into the floor. When he fell, the women ran out with great alarm, crying " *Lord amessy! Lord amessy!* " Doc went back home, cautiously put the rifle into its rack, and went to cutting wood again as calmly as if nothing had happened. Mrs. Evans told the Doctor that Doc had been doing *something*, that she saw him slip off with the rifle. The Doctor went out to the woodpile and asked —

" What have you been doing, son ? "

" Oh, nothing much ; — I 've just been down to Will Hill's."

" Did you shoot ? "

" Yes, sir."

" Did you kill anybody ?

" I don 't know ; — I shot at a man as he went into the house. When I shot he fell upon the floor, and the women all ran out crying."

" Are you not ashamed to do so cowardly a trick as that ? "

" No, sir. They slip up and shoot at us all night, and I thought I would pay them back a little this morning in their own coin."

It is not certain that the wound proved fatal, but not many days after that one of the Hill party was buried. This little incident cured the Hills of the habit of lying around the Doctor's house. It taught them that they were not safe, even if they were in a *fort*. Joe Murphy thought he would profit by the lesson and leave the country. Accordingly, he left his warlike clan and wound his way to some point on the Ohio river.

Dr. Evans learned this fact and sent William May, William Hogen, and Barnes Pendegrass, to bring him back. They caught and tied him, and delivered him into the county jail — thus securing the $200 reward offered by the Governor. There was only one room in the jail, and that the Evans boys occupied; hence he had to take the dungeon.

About this time, Mrs. Rus Hill came before the public to perform her part of the tragedy. She went up the creek one morning, telling every person she met that one of Isaiah and another of Fred Hill's boys had been shot dead in the yard, and that several shots came in at the door and wounded two or three of the little children. There was not a particle of truth in this. But she desired to raise a *breeze*, and, if possible, excite public feeling against Dr. Evans. She went to town and swore out a warrant against Dr. Evans and some thirteen others. One of the men named in the warrant was in Owen county at the time and never had any hand in the feud. They refused to go to Lancaster to have the trial, for they believed, as the neighbors affirmed, that it was a stratagem played to get a chance to kill the Doctor. To accommodate them, and to save the shedding of blood, Justice Ray held their trial in a little school-house near by, since known, from this fact, as 'Squire Ray's court-house. The accused were acquitted without any trouble, for the Hills had no evidence whatever to substantiate the accusation. When the sheriff went down to get Mrs. Hill to appear at the trial, he examined into the facts of the case and found it utterly false. The two boys were not killed, nor were the children wounded. Sam Hill had a small sore on his arm, which was believed to have been cut by Dr. Hill in order to give the woman's *tale* some shadow of truth.

Some thoughtless persons may look upon the conduct of Mrs. Hill with admiration, and deem it heroic and chivalric. Now, I am not prejudiced against Mrs. Hill, for I am acquainted with her only so far as her deeds have made her known. I have ever been an enthusiastic admirer of woman, that is, so long as she keeps within her proper sphere. But in the present case, I must confess, I do not see much to admire. Women naturally espouse the cause of their husbands, families, and friends, and often do valuable service, as did the women of the revolution, when they clothed and fed the naked and starving army that was fighting for liberty. In that instance we have much to admire, and much to tune the poet's lyre. Had they taken up arms, entered the field and fought for their country's rights, not only we would have sung their praise, but history would have shone with the splendor of the heroism till the end of all time. But suppose in the stead of thus feeding and clothing the destitute army, they had busied themselves in engendering and spreading false reports about the enemy's cruelty and wanton acts of violating chastity, to urge their husbands and brothers to atrocious deeds and unmitigated vengeance, the world would have ever detested them, for such conduct could leave only a stain upon history's page. We may admire Mrs. Hill for espousing the common cause of her party, but the manner in which she did it can but call down our bitter detestation. Had she become a modern Amazon, and defended herself and party with open arms, or by more equitable means, the ready pen and willing ink would have been glad to record her deeds ; but since she wielded only the blackest falsehoods and deception, they delineate with the slow solemnity of pity and commiseration. As advocates of morality, and enemies to vice, we should ever praise the one and denounce the other. She and her party would have more nearly accomplished their object by adhering to a straight-forward and honorable course. But " *anything* is fair in war," seems to have been their motto.

From that time, Dr. Evans began to stir about — before, he was afraid to leave home, for no one would have been there to protect his wife, had an attack been made. But there was little danger now, for the Hills had nearly all dispersed, and Dr. Hill was afraid to show himself. Though Dr. Hill was missing, he was not many miles distant, for one of his friends told Dr. Evans that he laid concealed in an old barn near Lancaster, and was fed by a negro.

The boys had quite a jolly time in jail. One day, to have a little sport, they showed the jailor where they could get out. He, to keep his prisoners safe, got some workmen with their sledge-hammers and went into repairing. While they were hammering away, creating a very disagreeable dust, one of the boys asked if they were going to close the window. They unthoughtedly replied in the affirmative. One of the boys then said, " Well, I'm going out of here ! "—at the same time taking hold of the door, and pulling it open. The jailer jerked the door, and they had a desperate struggle. He struck at Jack May with a knife, but Sam Evans drew a pistol and told him if he dared to cut Jack, that he would shoot him down. When they saw the pistol, the boys let loose the door and seized Sam, and all hallooed, " Don't shoot ! don't shoot ! " Quiet was soon restored, and Sam gave the pistol to the jailer. Before the trial was over, Tom Evans put the pistol into his boot-leg, and when he went to jail they did not search him on that part of his body, and he did not feel accommodating enough to inform on himself, so he carried it along. After they finished the repairs, the boys went to a log, raised it up, and showed another place through which they could escape, but the jailer thought they were safe enough as long as they remained thus honest. Some people believe they did this for mere sport, but others are of the more plausible opinion that the boys really intended to make their escape. I coincide with the latter, for about that time the Hills were committing great depredations on the Doctor's farm. This attempt to escape gave the Hills a fine theme for gossip, and aided by the influence of the Saulter family, they induced the jailer to send to the Governor for forty or fifty muskets and a strong guard to guard the jail. The Governor readily sent the guard, for it was represented to him that a mob was threatening to pull down the jail and take the boys out. There was a good deal of truth in this, for the people, not only in Garrard county, but in adjoining counties, talked seriously of demolishing the jail, for they believed it unjust to keep the boys thus imprisoned while Dr. Hill was roving at large. Many of the ladies too (God bless them) began to fire up with indignation at this apparent injustice, and said if the gentlemen did not pull down the jail that they would do it themselves. But Dr. Evans persuaded them not to be guilty of such a rash deed. He told them that the trial would soon come off, and the boys would then be free again ; that since the opposite party had resisted the law in every instance, he had resolved to pursue a different course ; that he feared nothing but the law, for it could not protect him, and prevented him from protecting himself. But the boys had quite a fine time, even if they were confined by double bolts and grating hinges. They employed their time principally over books, cards, newspapers, etc. The ladies, ever ready to soothe the sorrows of man, kept them well supplied with the dainties and luxuries of life, and not less with presents that fill the heart with gladness, and stir up the tender emotions of the soul.

The boys had their trial at the sitting of the November court. Before the trial came up, the Hill party and friends made a violent effort to adjourn the court, reporting that cholera had broken out very malignantly in town. But in spite of this effort the court continued — the boys were tried and acquitted. During the trial it was proven that Bedster had been hired to fight at fifteen dollars per month, with an extra pay of five dollars for every scalp taken from the Evans party. Bedster's mother threatened to sue Dr. Hill for his pay for services in this unholy war, but he went to see her and COMPROMISED the matter.

VARIOUS SKIRMISHES.

THE reader will perceive that Dr. Hill and Joe Murphy were left in rather an awkward position in the last chapter, one in the dungeon, and another concealed in an old barn; but from preceding events it could be well supposed that they were tried and readily acquitted.

From the fact that the Hills had been lying pretty close at Dr. Hill's for some time, Dr. Evans thought they had taken up their bivouac at some of the lower forts. Being thus persuaded, he anticipated little danger in sending Sam to town to see about some law-suits that were soon to come up. But to use a little precaution, Sam went late in the evening, with the intention of staying all night with his uncle Jesse,* who lived a few miles on the other side of town. From his uncle's, he could return to town, see his lawyers, and get away before the Hills were in the habit of going in. But as he was going into town that evening, he met Dr. Hill and David Russell walking on the pike a little distance from Hill's gate. As soon as Hill recognized Sam, he drew his pistol — Sam jerked his out instantly and fired. Dr. Hill, as if struck by the ball, jumped straight up, ran through the gate, got behind the gate-

---

* This was the only brother that Dr. Evans had in the country. But the Doctor would not permit him to participate in the fight in any manner what-ever, his motto being — " The fewer the better."

post, and fired back at Sam.   Sam ran his horse up to the post, and Hill ran away toward his house, under Sam's fire.   He ran about sixty yards then turned and fired again.

This is a miniature specimen of Dr. Hill's *brave* running. He was certainly practicing for the future, for these pages will certify that he arrived nearly to perfection in the art.   In his youthful days he doubtless imbibed and appreciated the sentiment : —

> " ' Tis better far to run away,
> And live to fight another day."

Sam rode on through town, and met Mr. Werret and told him what had happened.   As Sam wished to return the next morning, he requested Mr. Werret to keep a look-out and let him know if the Hills made any preparations.   He returned to Lancaster soon in the morning and stopped at the tavern, and there learned that the Hills were collecting all their forces. This piece of information was enough for him to know that it would be dangerous to venture homeward alone ; hence, he remained till he could get aid from home.   He wrote a letter to his father, requesting him not to come to town, for if he did, he would have to fight his way through.   But notwithstanding this, the Doctor, with three of his sons and William Murphy, set out with their rifles during the night.   They returned with Sam and passed Dr. Hill's house about daylight.   The Hills saw them and ran to give battle, but from some unknown cause paused and went back.

The next rencounter between Sam and Dr. Hill happened in Lexington.   It was on the memorable day of Henry Clay's funeral.   Sam went over on Friday and stopped at the McGowen House — the funeral did not come off till Saturday.   On Friday, Dr. Hill went down to some of the lower forts and learned that Sam had gone.   He ordered out his picket-guards to watch the river at the crossings for Sam's return, which was expected on the next evening.   After making these arrangements, he went back to Lancaster that night and hired a hack to take him to Lexington in the shortest possible time.   He arrived there about the middle of the day on Saturday, and took lodging also at the McGowen House.   His friends advised him to put up at some other house, for if he stopped there he might get into a difficulty with

7

Sam. He replied that he did not care for that. When he arrived, Sam had gone out to the cemetery, and not expecting to see an enemy, carried only his famous little revolver, leaving the large pistols in his saddlebags at the tavern. While at the cemetery, Sam was informed that Dr. Hill had arrived with several of his party, and would certainly give him battle. This did not at all please Sam's fancy, for he was not more than anxious to meet two or three well armed men, while he had only a small revolver. But, however, between two and three o'clock he concluded to go back to the tavern, even if it was occupied by a well armed enemy. When he arrived within about half a square of the tavern, he saw Dr. Hill, in company with two or three others, walking on the side-walk, and at the same time drawing his pistol. Sam instantly jerked out the little revolver, ran up and fired at his breast. The ball struck him but would not enter deeper than his clothes, on account, it is supposed, of an iron breast-plate. When Sam fired, Hill staggered back a few paces, then ran around a carriage which stood near by, then back on to the pavement. Sam snapped at him twice as he ran around. Hill ran down the pavement a short distance, but the dense crowd turned him into the more open street. Sam was in hot pursuit. When Dr. Hill got into the street, he fired a large pistol over his shoulder at Sam. The ball perforated a carriage and passed between a gentlemen and his lady. Dr. Hill made good use of his well trained legs, and according to the testimony of by-standers, ran faster than ever did the world-renowned " Grey Eagle," even in his prime. After running a considerable distance, Sam stopped and went back to the tavern. Hill got into his hack and started for home instantly, perhaps through cowardly motives, or to warn his stationed guards to be on the watch, but more probably to keep clear of the police. Sam got into a carriage with some of his friends and set out too, in a short time. Hill stopped on the road at Brown's to get his supper, but Brown told him that he expected Sam to be there in a few minutes to take supper. This was enough information for Hill, so he put off in post haste. He had just left, and had scarcely got out of sight when Sam drove up. Sam stopped at Brown's and took supper; then drove on. Hill went as far as Miller's then put up for the night. Though Sam knew he was there, he called at the house for a drink of water. It is very likely that the guards were sleeping on their posts, or lying in the ditch drunk, for Sam passed the river and arrived safely at home that night.

Now, reader, you will, doubtless, acquiesce in my former prediction, that Dr. Hill was training his legs at Lancaster for the glories of a future race. He won the race beyond doubt, and acquitted himself with a fame the least enviable. But, can you blame him, reader? Would you stand before a six shooter, even if it were in the hands of a strippling, and your breast plated over with impenetrable steel? I am inclined to think that some of us would feel a palpitation in the neighborhood of the left breast, and be strongly tempted to try the virtue of our legs. Dr. Hill was a very athletic man, and well knew how far to depend upon his physical powers. But being so well armed with large pistols, and protected securely by an impenetrable breastplate, it could have been hoped that he would have evinced more bravery and stood his ground before such a mere boy as Sam Evans was, and more so when he went there designedly to make the attack.

Dr. Evans and his wife were very uneasy about Sam, for they had learned the movements of Dr. Hill. According to an agreement with the boys, he was not to return by the way which he did, but to cross the river at the mouth of Paintlick creek, and stop at Gun's chapel, where a protracted meeting was then being held. The boys were also to meet him at this church, and keep a guard at the river to see if the Hills expected to waylay him there. This was about the time the people were trying to make a compromise between the two parties, for which reason the boys did not carry their rifles, as had been the case for some time. On Sunday morning, Dr. Evans sent a runner to tell the boys where the Hills were concealed in ambush; but the messenger never found the boys, nor returned, being afraid of the opposite party.

In the evening of the same day, a man went, in post haste, to get the boys' rifles at Dr. Evans's, and told the Doctor that the Hills had attacked Jack May's house, and dared him out to give them an open field fight. May unfurled a piece of red flannel to the breeze, and replied that he would give them an open field fight, or any other kind of a fight they desired, as soon as he could get ready. The boys, including Sam, were at May's house. When the guns arrived, May mustered his little company and marched out to where the enemy dared them. When the Hills saw the advancing foe, they retreated to a tobacco house at the extremity of the field. As the hindmost were going into the house, the boys got to the fence, whence the party had retreated, and fired upon them. In reply to this fire, some of them ran out and hallooed —

"D—n it, its too far to begin to shoot; — come over and give us an open field fight!"

The boys jumped over the fence and ran toward the house. This so frightened the Hills that they broke an opening through the back side of the house, and ran over to Fred Hill's house, leaving some of their guns. The boys gave them a hot chase and a shower of balls, though the distance was too great to do much execution.

Fred Hill's house was formed into a kind of fort, nailed up closely all round, save some little port holes through which to shoot. When the Hills got into it, they barred the door firmly, fearing the enemy would attempt to break in upon them. The boys approached pretty near the house, but by this time it was too dark for them to see to shoot. They hallooed to the Hills —

"You have Evans Bedster in there, and we want him — *we intend to have him!* The good citizens of Garrard have a process against him, and we are going to execute it. If you don't deliver him up, we will be so polite as to come in after him!"

A noise was then heard in the back part of the house as if they were breaking open a window and jumping out. The boys supposed they would aim to get to Clouse's house, and ran that way to intercept them. But unfortunately, or rather fortunately, the Hills happened to run the other way. They ran down to the river, waded across to an island, and concealed themselves under some trash or driftwood. The boys went to Clouse's and inquired for the Hills, but they had not been there. They then knew that they must be concealed somewhere under the cliff of the river. Hence, they kept a close watch about that place until noon on Wednesday, at which time a heavy rain fell and thoroughly wet them all, and spoiled their ammunition.

But the Hills laid as close as mice, and did not show themselves during the whole time, nor did they have a morsel of
food from Sunday night till noon on Wednesday. When the
boys left, the river rose rapidly on account of the heavy rain, and
threatened to overflow the island. Thus the proud Kentucky
sent her angry tides and disdainfully drove them from her do-
mains. They waded out, went up the river to the mouth of
Paintlick creek, up that creek to the mouth of Back creek, up
that to the mouth of Longbranch, and up that till they came to
the house of one of their relatives, and there stopped late in
the night to get something to eat. You may guess they were
a pretty hungry set of fellows, having fasted three days and
nights, and endured the severest exposure. After they had
eaten to their fill and rested, they set out for Lancaster and
arrived there about daybreak.

On Monday morning, while both parties were down on the
river, Mrs. Fred Hill went to Lancaster and swore out a warrant against the Evanses. *She swore that they had shot her
nose off* — shot into the house, into the skillet while she was
parching coffee and broke it, knocked the coffee pot over, and
done divers other *misdemeanors*. She went before the judge
with her nose tied up in a bundle of rags, with her eyes brimful
of tears, and swore that what she said was true.

In virtue of the warrant, the sheriff went down to Dr.
Evans's to get the boys. The Doctor told him that he had no
idea where the boys were; that they went to church on Sunday and had not been seen since, but that he expected them
home every day; and when they returned they would be at his
disposal, or that they would meet him on any day he might
choose. On the day appointed, the boys went to town to have
their trial, but not a Hill made his appearance, consequently
nothing was done. This was a fine joke on the judge; and the
people laughed at him heartily — *issuing a warrant for a lost
nose!* To secure future protection, the judge threatened to
prosecute them if they troubled him with any more of their false
swearing. In fact, her nose had nothing the matter with it,
but she bundled it up to make an *impression;* nor had any one
shot into the house. Her conscience, if not her nose, was
doubtless a fit subject for a government pension.

Now, as Dr. Evans and his party, numbering nine, were at Lancaster, and as the Hills, more than twenty strong, were collected at Fred Hill's house, every person thought they would have a desperate battle before they could get home. The Hills did not make use of this fine opportunity of meeting an unequal foe, but kept pretty close in their barracks. The Doctor kept a spy out to watch their moves till Saturday. The fact that they kept such close quarters induced the boys to believe that they were completely whipped—hence, on Sunday they scattered out to the different churches, thinking there would be no danger from the cowed enemy.

But the Doctor knew the wiles of the party better than to receive such an opinion. He believed they were waiting quietly only till the boys commenced to cut a certain piece of oats. The oatfield was in the form of a parallelogram, and bounded on three sides by a dense thicket and land belonging to Bill Hill. It was also within a few hundred yards of Hill's house, which rendered it very dangerous for the boys to work there. One morning, some of the boys went to cutting the oats, while the others, thinking there would be no danger, scattered out to different parts of the country. The Doctor stationed himself on one corner of the field where he could plainly see Hill's house and half a mile up and down the creek, and placed a spy at the other corner. The Doctor had not been at his post long before he saw seven or eight men at Hill's. They were more of the Washington troops, brought up by Bill Hill and Pat Williamson. In a short time, about a dozen of the *regulars* were seen marching up with their rifles, with Dr. Hill at their head. When they discovered Dr. Evans on guard, Dr. Hill pulled off his hat and waved it in the air, then leveled his gun as if in the act of shooting. They went on to the house and rested themselves under the shade trees. About this time the Doctor heard a loud noise and hallooing on the other side of his house. He turned and saw several men running down the hill from the barn toward the house, and hallooing — run! run! He did not understand the meaning of this, for they were strangers to him, but supposed them to be some of the raw recruits of the opposite party coming down to attack the house. The Doctor ran toward the house as fast as he could but they met him and told him that the Hills were preparing to attack the boys in the oatfield. They then ran on to give the boys the information. And the Doctor returned to his post. These men ran two or three miles in breathless haste, fearing the Hills would attack the boys unawares.

After the Hills rested a little time, they marched up the creek to a cornfield beyond the view of Dr. Evans. They had not been out of sight long before the report of a gun was heard, but it was some of the boys shooting as a signal for some of the others to shoot, so that they might know each other's locality, and thus get together. Some of the boys ran down to the creek and got into the old mill, expecting the Hills would pass near by it. But the miller made them go away, for he would have been in great danger had the two parties met there. They went back toward the oatfield into the thicket and discovered the Hills before they got into the cornfield — then the firing commenced. Two rounds were fired in quick succession by each of the parties. The Hills retreated across the creek and concealed themselves behind a clump of trees and the fence, still keeping up a brisk fire. But the fierce balls that came thick and fast from the opposite party made them retreat from behind their covert and run into Bill Hill's house. Some of them ran into the *smoke-house*, knocked out the *chinking*, and fired through the apertures between the logs. As soon as the Hills ran into the house the boys ceased firing, and hallooed to the women and children to come out and go away, for they intended to take the house by storm. The women cleared out like a flock of timid sheep, and went over to Mr. Harding's. The boys then went down closer to the creek and told the Hills to — " Come out and make one decisive battle. If you refuse, we will take the house by storm and compel you to fight. Come out and give us a fair fight, we will put our twelve men against your whole crew. *If you wont fight, we'll make you do it anyhow !* " This challenge was answered only by a hot fire from the house. Dr. Evans was still watching at his post, but not hearing the boys fire, became uneasy with the fear that some, of them were wounded, and started down to where they were. He met one of his sons who informed him that no one was hurt ; he therefore returned.

One of the Hills went out into the yard to hang up a coat on a
stick to see if the boys would shoot at it. About the time he
succeeded in fastening it to the pole, a gun fired from the
enemy's ranks and stretched him on the ground. He laid a
moment like a dead man, then crawled slowly into the house.
About twelve o'clock the boys ceased firing entirely, but the
fire from the house continued with unabated fury.

The Doctor then left his post to the care of two little
children, and went to the house to get his dinner. He found
about half of his party there — some eating, others moulding
bullets, making cartridges and fixing their cartridge boxes, as
if they intended to have a general campaign. The Doctor
asked where the other boys were. In reply, he was told
that they were lying out in the end of the oatfield asleep,
waiting for their dinners to be brought to them. When the
boys in the field got their basket dinner, they very hospitably
asked the Hills over to dine with them. But instead of a note
accepting the invitation, they received a shower of harmless
balls. After dinner the boys and the Doctor held a council of
war. At the conclusion of the consultation, the Doctor told
them — "You must not shoot at them any more at this
distance, it is only wasting ammunition. We must keep them in
the house till night, if possible, and then we'll *smoke 'em out*.
We must divide our company, and one half get on the brow of
the hill beyond the house ; and while the movement is making,
the party on this side must keep a big gun and fire at the
house to make them keep close that they may not perceive our
design. Then if they come out either way we will get them,
and give them a miniature Waterloo." According to the
Doctor's advice, while those that were to station themselves on
the opposite hill were going around the house, the remaining
party fired the Mississippi rifle into the house to make the Hills
keep dark, so that they would not perceive the move. The ball
fired into the house had more than the desired effect, for it tore
through the wall, went entirely through the house, making the
splinters and plaster fly, which dreadfully frightened the Hills.
They knew the report of the gun, and the desperate strength
with which she threw her balls ; and, to use their phraseology,
knew that it would be death to stand before the savage mouth

of old Mississippi. The second ball did even more execution than the first, and frightened them so much that they ran from the house to seek protection in the distance. Thus, the Doctor's plans were frustated. He wished to keep them there till night, but the terrible force with which the ounce balls shattered the walls, placed them in as much danger from the splinters as they would have been in an open field before the dreaded fire of the enemy. They ran out of the house and tried to conceal themselves in the green corn, but the balls of the foe could too easily search them under that fragile covering. They then ran back behind the house and got over the fence in double-quick time, each fellow taking care of his own head. As they were going up the hill, beyond gunshot, the boys discovered them and gave a close chase. The Hills ran over the hill and got out of sight before the boys could get up there.

The boys then returned toward home and met the Doctor. He told them that they could yet intercept the Hills, for they would certainly go one of two ways — either cross Davis's creek toward Mrs. Jenkins's, or down the creek to Mayfield's. He advised them to run across the country and secrete themselves on the way to Mrs. Jenkins's. They did so, and hid behind a log a few rods from the road. Before they started, they ordered two of the little boys to keep up a pretty constant fire to make the Hills believe they were not in pursuit. They also sent Thomas and James to a convenient point on the other road, with instructions to fire their guns if the Hills passed that way. They had not been seated in this ambush long before the Hill party came marching down the road, about two hundred yards distant. But, at this instant, the boys heard the reports of two guns, in quick succession, which they believed to be signals from Thomas and James, to indicate that the Hills were passing that way, hence, they sprang from their seats, ran in the direction of the reports, thus letting the Hills pass unmolested. This was a most thrilling incident. A gentleman on the adjacent hill side saw the boys concealed and the Hills advancing; he had pictured in his mind the horrors of the almost inevitable bloodshed; he heard the reports and saw the boys run away, which transported him with joy equal to his intense anxiety. Had the boys remained there only a few minutes longer, the

entire Hill party would have been slain, for the boys were numbered off so that each one would shoot at the man whose number corresponded with his own ; and, as the Hills were the more
numerous, the second round would be fired before they could
get ready to shoot, and those that remained then would fall before the small arms.   The guns were not fired as signals by
Thomas and James, but by the little boys in the field for the
deception of the Hills.

While the boys were firing at the house, a young man was
observed to get on his horse and slip slyly up the hill.   When
he got beyond the reach of the guns, he industriously applied
the whip to his horse and got away as quick as possible.   He
proved to be a young man by the name of Comely, who had
been drawn into the party, not by a love of battle, but by the
love of whisky and women.   He was pleased to stay with them
as long as he could get plenty to drink, but when the fighting
came up, he would rather be excused.   He went in post haste
to Lancaster and informed Mrs. Dr. Hill of the progressing
battle.   This news threw her into a wonderful phrensy ; — she
snorted around a considerable time trying to get some one to
accompany her to the battle ground.   But, finding none so gal-
lant as to become her escort, she set out alone and unprotected
upon the uncertain mission.   All nature was wrapt in the sable
mantle of night.   As she rode along in the invisible gloom, terrible thoughts and hobgoblins of the dreaded enemy preyed
upon her mind and chilled her frame with terror.   The roadside
was studded with hideous fiends, whose hellish eyes glared in
the darkness, and from whose throats issued blue flames and
dense sulphuric fumes, while their bloody teeth were gnashing
with impatience for the human victim.   She shuddered and
shrieked at the boundings and gnashings of these demons, but
the horse did not heed her agonies, and pursued, with steady
pace, the well known road.   The responsive shrieks of the
doleful night hawk she magnified to the war cry of the phan-
toms, as they engaged, in a hotly contested battle, to decide who
should be proprietor of her body.   At first, urged on by a feeling
of humanity, to dress the wounds of the living, and console the
last moments of the dying, she was now at the mercy of her
own imagination and the will of her faithful horse.   She dwelt

in the hell of her own mind. When the horse arrived at Hill's, he stopped at the accustomed block. She knew not where she was; she was lost in her own imagination. The reality of her position gradually displaced the bewilderment and she gained confidence to dismount. She slowly and cautiously approached the wide-spread door, but the cheerful prattle of innocent babes, as they gamboled before the fire, was hushed — the suppressed whisper of the more sagacious women was no more to be heard, and the clash of arms had long since died away — all was dark and dreary desolation. She stood a statue in the door; her heart ceased to beat; the dead silence seemed to tell a direful tale; the same fiery demons of her imagination clung to the walls, the ceiling, and stood thick in the impenetrable darkness, and hissed like serpents to augment her fright. She fled to her horse and retraced her ghost-infested journey. A kind negro offered a protecting hand and conducted her back home. When she arrived, she found the *heroes* of the late defeat standing at her gate.

THE CONCLUSION.

CHAPTER XIII.

Gabriel J. Saulter and Dr. Evans — Dr. Hill proposes to end the Feud — Peace declared — Disposal of the arms — Joe Murphy and John Brown ordered to leave the county — The Hill party leave the county — Murphy and Brown return and violate the treaty — Murphy goes to Lancaster and joins Dr. Hill — They arm themselves and search for Dr. Evans — Jack May kills Murphy — A stain upon the Evans party — Hills settle in Washington county — Fears that the Feud will be renewed — The moral.

AT Dr. Hill and Joe Murphy's trial for killing May, and before the acquittal had been pronounced, Gabriel J. Saulter, who was standing out in the square, sent for Dr. Evans. The Doctor went and mounted a block, with a crowd of people encircling him.

"Is there no way to put an end to this difficulty?" inquired Saulter.

"Yes," responded the Doctor; "if you would only resolve yourself into a committee of ways and means, you would soon find abundant ways. Your party can stop it whenever they wish ; all they have to do is to let me and mine alone. They started it, and must end it. At the time of the Lancaster fight, did you not say that you wished to see the Hills to make them quit fighting ? "

" I did say as much."

" Have they not always been your tools, your father's tools, and old John Hill's tools, with which you accomplished your dirty jobs ? "

" I will not say that they have been; — but they all love me ! "

" You could have made them quit fighting any time ; you could have prevented the Lancaster fight, but did not want to. You were not in earnest when you said you wished the fight to cease."

" I am in earnest, now ; I want, *really*, the fighting to end."

" If that is your desire. then say and do nothing more about it, and the whole affair is at an end. You have said everything you could to injure me and my family ; but, henceforth, treat me as a gentleman, and I will do the same by you and party."

" But it is reported about town that you intend to kill Dr. Hill and Joe Murphy, if they are cleared by the court."

" When, in the name of high heaven, will you and your babbling party quit lying ? You know as well as I do that there is not the shadow of truth in this. You know I never make an attack. But your party will spread any kind of a report that suits your purpose."

" Well, never mind that — let us come to some conclusion. To show you that I am in earnest, I will sign that petition to the Governor to remit Sam's fine, and will take it to Dr. Hill and get him also to sign it."

Saulter was in earnest this time, and it is believed that he did everything in his power to end the Feud. The next morning after the conversation, Hamilton Duggins, one of Dr. Hill's particular friends, went to see Dr. Evans.

" Dr. Hill sent me over here," said Duggins, " to inform you that he wants to quit fighting. He only wants you to *say* that you will quit, for he believes you will do what you say. He will dispose of his weapons in any way you may desire."

" You may tell Dr. Hill," replied Dr. Evans, " if that is his desire, he has nothing more to do than to quit. If he will now declare peace, and observe the stipulations, he and party shall never be disturbed by me and mine. So far as his arms are concerned, those that he stole at the Scott's fork tragedy, must be returned to their owners. The big shot-gun belongs to me, the little rifle to James Lane, who has had no hand in the fight, and the pistol and bowie-knife to the widow Chrismon. Those that he borrowed from his neighbors must be returned; for, if he is like me, he has enough of his own to quit fighting with. Those that he has bought and *paid* for, he is at liberty to do with as he pleases — he can either sell them, wear them, or break them."

A few days after this, Dr. Hill wrote a long letter to Dr. Evans, entrusting the delivery of the same to George Smith and Gabriel Saulter. These latter gentlemen were on the way to execute their mission one morning, but met the Doctor in the road, not far from Lancaster, and made known their business. The letter made all the acknowledgments and admissions that could be desired, save with respect to the disposal of the guns. But it also contained information that Smith and Saulter were the authorized agents of the Hill party, and they had power to modify any of the propositions. They agreed that the guns should be returned or paid for, and that Joe Murphy and John Brown should leave the county immediately. But Murphy was to have the liberty of returning, in the following spring, to attend his trial for killing a negro woman.

The majority of the Hill party immediately left the county, and the others were making preparation to follow the example. But Murphy and Brown soon came back, settled on Paintlick creek, and swore they intended to go where they pleased. In direct violation of the treaty, they drew a boundary line between themselves and the opposite party, and swore that the penalty would be death for any of them to cross the line. They not only made threats, but put them into execution — for they did actually waylay the Doctor, as he went to Teetersville to attend to some business. It is supposed that they did this not on their own account or desire, but because ordered to do so by Dr. Hill. These daring acts emboldened them to rasher deeds, and induced them to take ambuscade even in their old battle ground, on Sugar creek. These facts will serve to show how faithfully Dr. Hill observed the treaty, though ne was all the time pretending to be preparing to move to California.

On one bright morning, when the sun shone gladly forth, and the azure tints of the sky seemed to grow deeper with joy at the happy peace that had been concluded, Joe Murphy sauntered about his log cabin, with an air that bespoke the contemplation of some dire event. He was the personification of discontent. The sublimity of the high limestone hills, that embowered his little hut, aided by the unparalleled serenity of the weather, seemed not to have a cheering influence upon his heart. He was feverishly gloomy and morose, and devoured his rude breakfast with an absence of mind and heavy drawn sighs. After hastily swallowing the morning repast, he told his wife that he intended to go away and never return. His wife entreated and implored him not to be guilty of so rash and woful a deed. But his reckless heart was dead to all the influences of love and the tender endearments of home; her wailings were answered only by the echo of the surrounding hills and extended forest; he tore himself away, never again to see her whom he had loved.

He went immediately to Lancaster in this frenzied mood and joined Dr. Hill. They wildly indulged the maddening fires of intoxicating liquors. Being frantic with the fire that stimulated their giddy brains, they buckled on their oft-worn armor, and sallied forth into the town to seek whom they could devour. As chance would have it, Dr. Evans and some of his friends happened to be in town that day, but were soon informed of the approach of the enemy. The Doctor believed the entire Hill party to be concealed in town, from the actions of Joe Murphy, who attempted, several times, to get a shot at the prime object of the war. This frightened the Doctor, and to prevent any more bloodshed, he thought it advisable to leave for home.

After the Doctor left, Joe Murphy laid away his weapons and seated himself quietly before the tavern fire. Not many hours had rolled into the forgetful past, when Jack and Bill May, two of the Evans party, on pretence to get a drink of liquor, went over to the tavern. When Jack May entered the room and saw Murphy sitting before the fire, he drew a revolver, put it against the temple of Murphy's head, and shot two balls through his brain. He fell dead upon the floor !

This certainly was the blackest deed committed by the Evans party. They had hitherto professed too much nobleness of heart to waylay the enemy or sneak up behind them unawares ; but now we see their policy violated, at the conclusion of the contest, and upon an unarmed and defenceless man. Thus we see them do that which they had preached against for years. Prior to this time, they conducted themselves admirably, but this last act was the most cruel of all. Who can divine the hypocritical workings of the human heart! I do not say that this is an immediate stain upon Dr. Evans's family, for, perhaps, the Doctor would not have countenanced the deed before committed. Nor do I say that they were not justifiable in the act; for the Hills had already broken the treaty in returning and attempting to shoot Dr. Evans ; and when an obligation is broken by one of the bound parties, it cannot bind the other. But, having been such advocates of open and fair work, we should have hoped that they would not be guilty of this low trick. Though the Mays went to the tavern, under pretext of getting a drink of liquor, some people are of opinion that the whole affair was preconcerted and advised by Dr. Evans. We have no proof of this, but every one is at liberty to enjoy his own opinion. It is enough to make us doubt that the Evanses were actuated to their honorable course of conduct by principles of honor, and make us believe that they aimed only at public applause. But the misdeed of one individual should not rest upon the entire party, much less upon Dr. Evans's family, for one might do what the whole would condemn.

When Murphy fell, May ran across the square, got his horse and left immediately. When the news reached Dr. Hill, who was on the opposite side of town, he exclaimed with great excitement —

" Who will now say that I had better not leave this county ? Every breath I breathe here is fraught with danger ! "

The tavern keeper sent word to Dr. Hill to know what should be done with Murphy's body. He replied —

" By G—d, I 'm afraid to do anything with him. I gave the d—d fool money to go off on, and now as he has come back, I will have nothing to do with him ; and the Evanses would rather kill me than Joe Murphy any day, were they to get a chance."

Murphy was taken down to his brother's, and buried the next

evening.   Dr. Hill and John Brown, the last of the party, left
the country as soon as they could get away.

Here, reader, end the scenes of this bloody and exciting
Feud — and gladly do I end it.   You have the facts before
you, and can reflect upon them in your own peculiar style.   The
Hills all left the neighborhood, and the majority of them moved
to Washington county, where they now reside.   They were a
most distressed party, composed mostly of helpless widows and
their numerous families of little, destitute children.   They were
truly objects of charity.   It is uncertain in what land Dr. Hill
chose to make his home, but it is believed he went into Tennes-
see and continued the practice of his profession.

Some people believe that the Feud has not yet ended, but
that when the numerous children of these families become a
little older, they will rise and avenge the blood of their fathers.
But it may be hoped that Kentucky will not meet this horrible
fate; for the tomahawk has long since been buried under the
tree of peace, and the green grass of forgetfulness has grown
thick over it.   The memory of past wrongs may yet cause, in
the surviving Hills, heart-burnings, but the history of the past
warns them to value the peace and safety they now enjoy.   The
past is dark and the future bright to them, and they will be
slow to call down again upon themselves the miseries once
experienced.   The past stands to them a warning and a guide.

This narrative is not devoid of a moral.   The reader has
before him two parties : the one, acting honorably and on the
defensive ; the other, using every unfair means on the offensive.   He sees the just come off victorious and with honor,
while the unjust is vanquished and compelled to flee the country in disgrace.   He can view the one course with admiration,
the other with detestation, and can choose between them in his
own affairs.   It clearly proves that, he who pursues an honest
and honorable course, will, in the end, be triumphant over every
obstacle, and rise above every attempt at oppression.

Made in the USA
Middletown, DE
10 September 2018